A Drop of Irish Jokes

Published in 2005 for
Lagan Books

by
Appletree Press Ltd
The Old Potato Station
14 Howard Street South
Belfast, BT7 1AP

Tel: +44 (0) 28 90 24 30 74
Fax: + 44 (0) 28 90 24 67 56
E-mail: reception@appletree.ie
Web-site: www.appletree.ie

Design & Layout © Appletree Press Ltd, 2005

A Drop of Irish Jokes

ISBN: 0 86281 982 2

Desk & Marketing Editor: Jean Brown
Editor: Jim Black
Design: Stuart Wilkinson
Production Manager: Paul McAvoy

9 8 7 6 5 4 3 2 1

AP3278

Dedicated to Irishmen and Irishwomen all over the world.

A Drop of Irish Jokes

Terry Adlam

LAGAN BOOKS

Liam saw Shaun walking down the road carrying two house bricks.

'Where you going with the bricks?' asked Liam.

'I'm going round O'Malley's house,' answered Shaun.

'What for?' Liam questioned.

'Well last night, O'Malley put a brick through my window,' said Shaun. 'So I'm going round to do the same to his window.'

'Oh right,' said Liam. 'But why two bricks?'

'Because,' replied Shaun, 'O'Malley's got double glazing.'

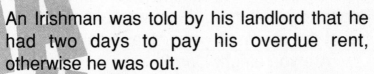

An Irishman was told by his landlord that he had two days to pay his overdue rent, otherwise he was out.

'Fine,' said the Irishman. 'Can I have Easter Sunday and Christmas Day?'

Liam and Shaun were mountain climbing, when Liam suddenly fell into a 400 feet deep crevasse.

'Liam, you alright?' shouted Shaun.

'I'm alive!' called Liam.

'Great,' called a relieved Shaun, 'I'll throw you a rope. Grab it and I'll pull you up.'

'I can't grab it,' shouted up Liam. 'I've broken both my arms.'

'Fit it around your legs, then,' instructed Shaun.

'Can't do that either,' said Shaun. 'I've broken my legs as well!'

'Well put the rope in your mouth,' Shaun called.

So Liam put the rope in his mouth and Shaun began to pull him up. Liam was almost at the top of the crevasse when Shaun called out.

'Are you alright Liam?'

Liam said, 'Yea..h..hhhhhhhhhhhhhhhhhhhh!'

Mary and Colleen met in a wine bar, ordered a drink and sat down at a nearby table.

'So, asked Mary, 'how's your husband?'

'Compared to what?' replied Colleen.

An Irishman is backing his car into his garage, when he runs over his cat, Rover, and kills it stone dead. Next to the ex-cat is a lamp. The Irishman picks up the lamp and rubs it, and sure enough a genie appears. Not a very big one, more of a teenie genie. Anyway the genie grants him one wish.

'Bring Rover back to life, please,' asks the Irishman.

'I'm so sorry,' says the teenie genie. 'That wish is just too difficult to grant.'

'OK, what about her?' says the Irishman, pointing to his wife who is sitting in the car.

'What about her?' questions the teenie genie.

'Make my wife beautiful.'

The teenie genie takes a look at the Irishman's wife then says, 'Hang about, let me have another look at that cat.'

They had a comedy night in the local pub and an Irishman wasn't impressed because of all the Irish jokes being told. By the time of the last act he had had enough.

'Oy,' shouted the Irishman. 'Stop the Irish jokes. You're making us all out to be a bunch of stupid eejits. In fact, if you tell another Irish joke, I'm coming up there and I'm gonna knock yer block off.'

Obviously taken aback the ventriloquist started to apologise. 'I'm very sorry...'

'You keep out of it!' shouted the Irishman. 'I'm talking to the little fella on yer knee.'

Liam found Shaun painting a window frame so furiously that he was making a mess of it.

'Shaun, take it easy,' said Liam. 'Why are you working so fast?'

'I'm trying to finish this window frame before the paint runs out,' replied Shaun.

Mary went to the local police station to report that her husband was missing.

'OK,' said the desk sergeant, not looking up. 'Let's have a few details. What was he like?'

'Well,' began Mary, 'he was 27 years old, 6ft 2", he had long dark wavy hair and he was absolutely drop dead gorgeous.'

'I see,' replied the desk sergeant, looking up from his note and instantly recognising Mary. 'Wait a minute, you're Mary. I know your husband. He is fat, short, balding and over 50 years old.'

Mary looked crestfallen. 'I know,' she said, 'but sure who'd want *him* back?'

Finnegan had died and as he lay at rest at home, friends and family came to pay their last respects.

'It's so sad,' said one friend to his grieving widow, 'and yet he looks so happy.'

'I know,' said the wife, 'Finnegan always was slow on the uptake.'

'What do you have in that bag?' asked Liam when he met his mate Shaun.

'Chickens,' said Shaun.

'If I guess how many there are in the bag,' said Liam, 'can I have one?'

'If you guess how many there are in the bag, you can have both of them.'

A couple were visiting a small village just outside Kerry and admiring its traditional setting and ways. The wife approached a strange-looking yokel leaning up against a gate.

'Excuse me,' she said politely. 'This village is so rural and well, so traditional, I was wondering if you still have a village idiot?'

The yokel looked at her and shook his head. 'Ah now Missus, I'm afraid we don't have a single village idiot at all at all.'

'Oh,' said the wife, disappointed.

'No,' continued the yokel, 'we all take it in turns.'

Building site foreman, Ivor C. Mentmixer, was very worried when his top Irish brickie, told him that if he didn't give him a rise he would have to leave, owing to the fact that he had three other companies after him. Ivor was less worried when he found out that the companies were the Gas Board, the Electricity Board and the Water Board.

It was the Dublin Winter Olympics and the Bulgarian skater Onmebum Mostofdatime raced on the ice rink and promptly fell over.

Ever the professional, the skater got to his feet and continued his routine in a disastrous way, falling over more times than he stood up.

At the end of the routine he received no points from any of the judges, apart from the Irish judge who gave him 8.5 points.

When the Irish judge was asked by a confused official why he had scored the skater so high, he replied, 'Well, he did well. Sure it's ever so slippery out there.'

A young Irish boy comes racing home to his mammy very excited.

'Mammy, Mammy,' he squealed. 'You'll never believe it, but I was walking past the baker's and guess what I saw?'

'What did you see?' asked his old mammy.

'I only saw that they had made cakes with my signature on them.'

Old mammy was curious. 'Did they now. And did you buy one?'

'I did better that that Mammy, I bought two. Look!'

He opened the bag he was carrying and his old mammy looked in.

'Oh yes, that's very nice darling. Some people call them Hot Cross Buns.'

SPORTS NEWS!
The inaugural Irish steeplechase was finally abandoned this afternoon because the horses couldn't get a decent grip on the church roof.

Famous theatrical agent, Arthur Noon-Matinee was walking past a Galway building site when he saw Paddy perform a double somersault off some scaffolding, a back flip off a pile of bricks, a cartwheel over a cement mixer and execute a perfect landing. Arthur went rushing up to the Site Manager, introduced himself and said that he must book Paddy for a forthcoming show.

'You'll have to book Thaddy as well,' said the Site Manager.

'Why is that?' asked Arthur.

'Because,' said the Site Manager, 'Thaddy was the one who hit Paddy's thumb with the sledgehammer.'

An Irishman was in a shopping centre when he saw a sign: 'Dogs must be carried up the escalator'.

He spent the next two hours looking for a dog!

Dermot O'Toole was an actor from Dublin of limited range and had been out of work, or as he called it "Resting, Darling," for quite a long time.

Then one day his agent rang to say he had got him a part in a play with a Belfast Theatre Company. The part only had one line, but it could be the break that O'Toole was looking for.

O'Toole took the job and began rehearsing straight away. The line was 'Hark, is that a cannon I hear?'

He rehearsed the line on the way to the station in the taxi: 'Hark, is that a cannon I hear?' He repeated the line over and over again on the journey to Belfast and in the cab to the theatre: 'Hark, is that a cannon I hear?'

He was still repeating it when he was shown to his dressing room and as he got into his costume.

'Hark, is that a cannon I hear?'

'Hark, is that a cannon I hear?'

There was a knock on his door. 'Five minutes Mr O'Toole!' called the Stage Manager.

'Hark, is that a cannon I hear?' O'Toole continued calmly.

A while later there was another knock. 'One

minute, Mr O'Toole.' O'Toole rehearsed and rehearsed: 'Hark, is that a cannon I hear?'

'Hark, is that a cannon I hear?' he repeated over and over as he walked from his dressing room to the stage and one more time in the wings just before he was about to go on stage.

Then his moment came. O'Toole strode on to the stage and there was a blinding flash and an enormous bang.

'Oh Bejasus!' he shouted. 'What the divil was that?'

An Irishman walked into his local barbers and asked how much a haircut was.

'Five pounds,' said the barber.

The Irishman thought for a while and then asked, 'How much for a shave?'

'That's only a pound,' replied the barber.

'OK then,' said the Irishman, 'shave me head.'

An Irishman saw a man on a bridge about to jump off, so he rushed up to him.

'Don't jump man! Think of your wife and children.'

'I've haven't got a wife or children,' said the man.

'Well, think about your parents?'

'I'm an orphan.'

'Well then, think of St Patrick.'

'Who's St Patrick?' asked the man.

That was when the Irishman pushed him.

Paddy was visiting Pat in hospital. Pat had broken nearly every bone in his body and was covered, apart from his mouth, from head to toe in plaster.

'Blimey Pat,' said Paddy, 'your parachute jump didn't go that well, did it?'

'No,' groaned Pat.

'What happened?' asked Paddy.

'Me parachute didn't open,' Pat mumbled.

'Oh dear!' commiserated Paddy. 'You should have got an Irish parachute. You know, the ones that open on impact.'

Mr and Mrs O' Rourke were on holiday in Spain and they kept hearing the expression 'Manyana.' So they asked their guide Juan Phorderoad what it meant.

"Mañana',' began Juan, 'translates as, "Maybe the job will be done soon, maybe tomorrow, maybe the next day, maybe the day after that. Perhaps even next week, or month or year, who cares?" 'Mañana'.'

'Well now, that's very interesting!' said Mrs O'Rourke.

Juan smiled. 'Tell me, do you have a similar expression in Ireland?'

'No,' said Mr O'Rourke, 'we rarely have that degree of urgency.'

Now, no one is saying that O'Malley was tight with money, but he did get rid of his barometer when he found out his wife had flu. When she had a temperature of 110 degrees Fahrenheit, he put her in the cellar to heat the house up!

An Irishman was sent out by his wife to get some edible snails for a dinner party they were having that evening, Off he went and bought about a dozen, then on the way home he popped into his local for a quick one, or two, or three or…

Well, come closing time, he had had more than enough and had missed the dinner party. On his wobbly way home he knew he was in big trouble. Sure enough when he got home he looked through the letterbox and there was his wife waiting for him, and she wasn't looking too happy.

So the Irishman put the snails on the doorstep and opened the door saying loudly:

'Now come on lads, hurry up, otherwise I'm in big trouble.'

Did you hear the one about the Irishman who tried to repair a gas leak in his local hospital?

Doctors informed his wife that he was on a life support machine, a bed, the curtains, the ceiling, the windows…

A group of young Irish boys had formed their own ten-piece Rhythm and Blues band and were playing their first gig. The lead singer was very excited by the event and asked one of the sax players to go outside and listen to what they sounded like.

Sure enough the saxophonist went outside and after while came running back, very excited. 'You should hear it!' he said excitedly. 'It sounds brilliant!'

So the whole band went out to listen…

A holidaymaker was making his way to the bathroom in Mary's bed and breakfast.

'Excuse me, Sir,' Mary said. 'Do you have a good memory for faces?'

The holidaymaker stopped at the bathroom door and said, 'Yes I do actually.'

'That's great,' said Mary, 'because there's no mirror in the bathroom.'

Shaun met Liam and asked, 'Have you seen O'Riley lately?'

'A good question,' said Liam, 'because I have and I haven't.'

Shaun was confused (well wouldn't you be?).

'What do you mean by that?'

'Well, I was walking down the road the other day,' began Liam, 'and I saw someone who I thought was O'Riley, and he said that he thought he saw someone he thought was me. But when we got up close... it was neither of us.'

Mary and Colleen were enjoying another glass of wine and a chat in another winebar:

'For his birthday, my husband wants to go somewhere he's never been to and do something he's never done before,' said Mary.

'So where are you sending him?' asked Colleen.

'To the kitchen to do the ironing!' said Mary.

An Irishman came home looking very upset.

'What's up?' asked his wife.

'I've been sacked from me job on the one-man bus,' he said.

'Why?' his wife questioned.

'Because the bus crashed and they said it was my fault.'

'What happened?'

'I don't know,' replied the Irishman. 'I was upstairs collecting fares at the time.'

Moylan noticed that Doylan was looking very sad as they met in the street.

'What's the matter?' asked a concerned Moylan.

'I've lost me dog,' moaned Doylan, 'and I can't find him.'

Moylan said, 'Why don't you put an advert in the local paper?'

Doylan stared at Moylan in bewilderment. 'Don't be daft. You know he can't read.'

Liam was watching Shaun dig a hole in his garden.

'Shaun,' called Liam 'where are you going to put all that soil when you've dug that hole?'

'I'm going to dig another hole and put it all in that,' Shaun smugly replied.

'Ya eejit,' laughed Liam. 'Then you'll have all the soil from *that* hole left over.'

'No I won't,' answered Shaun even more smugly than the last time, 'because I'm going to dig that hole much deeper.'

Two Irishmen were playing snooker together for the first time. They had been playing for nearly two hours without potting a single ball and thoroughly enjoying themselves when one of them whispered,

'Do you think we should take that wooden triangle off the balls?'

A little Irish girl had lost her mammy in a busy supermarket and was crying.

'What's the matter?' asked a friendly shop assistant.

'I've lost me mammy!' bawled the little Irish girl.

'Now, now, don't worry,' said the friendly shopkeeper. 'We'll find her. Now tell me, what's she like?'

The little Irish girl stopped sobbing, and said, 'Bingo, Coronation Street, Tom Jones, Dad going away on business...'

'So,' said Arthur Noon-Matinee the well-known theatrical agent to an Irishman, 'You do bird impressions.'

'That's right, Sir,' replied the Irishman.

'And what do you do exactly?' Sir Arthur asked. 'Nightingale, Skylark, Chaffinch?'

'No Sir,' said the Irishman. 'I eat worms.'

A man burst into the bank brandishing a firearm and screamed at the teller behind the counter.

'Hand over all the money. Do it quick and no one will get hurt.'

'You're Irish, aren't you?' enquired the unperturbed bank clerk.

'Yes!' said the Irishman. 'How did you know?'

'You've sawn off the wrong end of your shotgun,' came the calm reply.

An Irishman was sitting in the park enjoying some fish and chips when a woman with a small dog sat next to him. The dog could smell the fish and chips and got quite excited and kept jumping up at the Irishman and yelping.

'Excuse me, Miss,' said the Irishman. 'Do you mind if I throw your dog a bit?'

'Not at all,' smiled the woman. So the Irishman picked up the dog and threw it into the duck pond.

A man went into an Irish optician to complain about his failing eyesight so the Irish optician took him outside and pointed up into the sky.

'What can you see up there?' he asked.
The man looked up and replied, 'the sun.'
The Irish optician said, 'Well, how far do you want to see?'

Freddy O'Flipper trained hard to become the first Irishman to swim the Irish Sea and the day came when he was ready. Things started off well and Freddy swam hard and strong. Halfway across the sea he was tired but still determined. This determination carried him onwards, but unfortunately with the shore just in view Freddy was exhausted. There was just no way he was going to make it. Disappointed, he turned around and swam home.

Tom walked into Mick Kanic's garage and said, 'Mick, I've got a problem with my car.'

'What is it?' asked Mick.

'It's a form of transport powered by an internal combustion engine,' answered Tom.

'No,' sighed Mick, 'I meant, what's the matter with your car?'

'Oh, there's water in the carburettor,' replied Tom.

'We'll soon get that sorted out,' smiled Mick confidently. 'Where's your car?'

'The fire brigade are just fishing it out of the river as we speak,' said Tom.

A little Irish girl was in class learning the alphabet, when her teacher asked her:

'So, what comes after 'T'?'

'The Six O'clock News!' the little Irish girl replied.

Two Irishmen had decided to take up duck hunting. So off they went on their first shoot. Eight hours passed and not one duck had they bagged.

'This duck hunting isn't as good as it's made out to be,' said one of them. 'We've been here all day and what have we got? Nothing. That's what!'

'I know,' agreed the other one. 'Do you think we're not throwing the dog high enough?'

Sweethearts Geri and Terry were sitting on a park bench bathed in the romantic sheen of moonlight.

'If I won the Lotto,' began Geri, 'I'd get myself a new house and a new swimming pool and a new car and a new motorbike and a new boat, and a new wardrobe of clothes, and...'

'Darling,' Terry softly interrupted, 'what about me?'

'...a new boyfriend,' continued Geri.

An Irishman rang up the Guinness Book of Records to tell them that he had just completed a 1000 piece jigsaw in three weeks. 'It must be a world record!' he said excitedly.

'Why do you think that?' asked the man from the Guinness Book of Records.

'Because on the box it says "two to five years".'

'This is a very unusual chair,' the Irishman said to his dentist. 'Most dentist's chairs go up and down, don't they? This one just goes backwards and forwards. It's quite unusual.'

Then the dentist said, 'Mr O'Malley, please get out of the filing cabinet.'

An Irishman was at his Mammy's house and noticed a number of empty milk and beer bottles in his fridge.

'Mammy,' asked the Irishman, 'why are there empty milk bottles in the fridge?'

'Ah,' said his Mammy, 'that's just in case anyone comes round and wants a black coffee.'

'What about the empty beer bottles?' the Irishman asked again.

'They're for people who come round who don't drink.'

An Irishman hobbled out of a Dublin hospital on crutches, with both his legs in plaster. He met his friend, who was going into the hospital for the results of his dope test, and his friend stopped him.

'Hey!' he said. 'What happened to you?'

'I've broken both my ankles,' said the Irishman. 'That's the last time I try to make my own coconut wine.'

Have you heard the one about the new Irish video recorder?

It records the programmes you don't want to see, and shows them when you're out!

It was announced on television recently that Delia O'Burnt-it the famous Irish TV chef had got fed up making chocolate chip cookies. Apparently it took her too long to peel the Smarties.

Did you hear the one about the Irish schoolboy who was a bit on the thick side?

When he was at school he always used to play truant two days a week. Then he found out that the other kids didn't go to school on Saturdays and Sundays either!

An Irishman got a job on the dustcarts. It was a job he picked up quite quickly. In fact he was so good, that he could carry a bin under each arm and balance another one on his head. One day his friend saw the Irishman carrying all his bins and whistling happily.

'Wow,' said his friend. 'That's fantastic. How do you do it?'

'It's easy,' grinned the Irishman. 'I just puts me lips together and blow.'

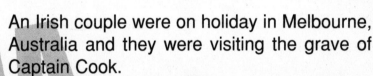

An Irish couple were on holiday in Melbourne, Australia and they were visiting the grave of Captain Cook.

'I wonder how he died?' asked the wife. The husband thumbed through the guidebook and found the appropriate page. 'It says here that he was murdered.'

'I'm not surprised,' replied his spouse, 'especially after what he did to Peter Pan and Wendy!'

Liam looked up from his *Book of Interesting Facts* and turned to Shaun. 'It says here that a camel can go for five hundred miles without water.'

'That's amazing,' gasped Shaun, 'can you imagine how far he could go *with* water!'

Did you hear the one about the Irish boy who arrived home one day carrying a settee under one arm and an armchair under the other?

His mammy told him off for taking suites from strangers!

An Irish girl went to see her doctor, Dr R.U. Inpain with a very baldly burnt ear. 'How on earth did that happen?' enquires the doctor.

'Well,' says the Irish girl, 'I was doing the ironing when I heard the phone ring...'

An Irishman went up to the counter in a shop.

'I'd like *Shrek 2* please.'

'I'm sorry, Sir,' said the shopkeeper, 'but this is a fish and chip shop.'

'Oh?' said Irishman. 'I'll have *A Fish Called Wanda*, then.'

'So children,' smiled the teacher. 'Can you name six animals that come from Africa?'

'Sure can, Miss,' beamed the confident little Patrick. 'An elephant, a lion and four giraffes.'

A young Irish boy was watching his father whittle away at a piece of wood in his workshop.

'What you making, Daddy?' asked the little Irish boy.

'A portable,' replied his father.

'A portable what?' asked the little Irish boy again.

'I don't know yet,' said the Irishman. 'I've only just made the handle.'

An Irishman went into a men's clothes shop and spoke to the assistant behind the counter.

'Excuse me, but I'd like to return this tie and get my money back.'

'No problem, Sir,' said the Assistant. 'Didn't you like the colour?'

'No,' replied the Irishman. 'It was too tight.'

An Irishman went into his local fish shop 'In Cod We Trust' late one night, and asked the owner if he could borrow twenty pounds.

'I'm afraid you can't,' said the owner, 'on account of the arrangement I have with the bank.'

'What arrangement?' asked the Irishman.

'They don't sell fish and chips and I don't lend money,' replied the owner.

Paddy saw Thaddy digging a hole in his garden.

'What're you doing?' asked Paddy, noticing that the garden was already covered with a number of other holes.

'My dog died,' said Thaddy, wiping his brow, 'so I'm digging a hole to bury him in.'

'So what are those other holes for?' enquired Paddy.

'They were other holes I'd dug to bury the dog in,' replied Thaddy, 'but they weren't big enough.'

Did you hear the one about the Irishman who enrolled at night class?

He thought they would teach you to read in the dark!

A white horse trots into a Dublin pub and orders a drink.

'Hey!' says the Barman. 'We've got a whiskey named after you.'

'What, Dobbin?' said the horse.

Mary and Colleen were enjoying yet another glass of wine and a chat in another local wine bar.

'I read somewhere,' said Colleen, 'that bigamy is when you are married to one man too many.'

Mary sighed. 'I would say that monogamy is very much the same.'

An Irish landlord was very concerned when the brewery told him that they couldn't deliver any stout to his bar.

He knew that if he didn't do something he would lose customers and money. So he came up with a brilliant idea. He gave all his regulars sunglasses and served them lager!

An Irishman went into a pizza restaurant and ordered a pizza with all the trimmings. When it was ready the cook asked, 'Do you want me to cut it into four or eight slices?'

The Irishman thought for a while and then said, 'Best cut it into four slices – I'll never be able to eat eight.'

Did you hear the one about the Irishman who was caught illegally importing cheap Irish workers into Ireland?

He was found guilty of dope smuggling!

Mary and Colleen were enjoying a glass of wine and a chat in their local wine bar 'The Grapes of Waterford.'

'My husband says that if there is such thing as reincarnation, he wouldn't mind coming back as a pig,' said Mary.

'What did you say to that?' asked Colleen between sips.

'I told him that wouldn't happen, because you have to come back as something different.'

Having done the football pools for many, many years, an Irishman was very excited when a man from Littlewoods finally knocked on his front door.

'Does this mean I've won the Pools?' asked the very excited Irishman.

'No,' replied the man from Littlewoods. 'We've just caught your wife shoplifting.'

An Irishman was in his local butchers and fishmongers, 'Whale Meat Again', when a great big Alsatian bounded in and snapped up a couple of pounds of sausages from the counter and ran off.

'Hey!' shouted the butcher to the Irishman. 'Wasn't that your dog?'

'He was,' replied the Irishman calmly, 'but he fends for himself these days.'

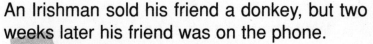

An Irishman sold his friend a donkey, but two weeks later his friend was on the phone.

'That donkey you sold me?'

'What about it?'

'It's just dropped dead.'

'Has it?' replied the surprised Irishman. 'It never did that when I had it.'

A young Irishman brought three girls home to meet his Mammy.

'Mammy, I'm getting married to one of these lovely girls. Can you tell which one?'

'The one in the middle!' she said straight away.

The young Irishman was shocked.

'Mammy, that's amazing. How did you know?'

'I don't like her,' snarled his Mammy.

'Well, how did you get on?' asked an Irishman's wife when he returned home from a job interview with a well-known German car manufacturer.

'I didn't get the job,' sighed the Irishman.

'Why not?' said the Irishman's wife.

'I couldn't spell BMW.'

An Irishman rang his wife up in a very excited state.

'Get packing... I won the Lotto!' he screamed.

His wife was obviously delighted.

'Wow, that's great news. I'll start right away. What shall I pack? My summer clothes for a tropical holiday or my skiwear or something glamorous?'

'Pack what you like,' said the Irishman. 'Just make sure you are out of the house when I get home.'

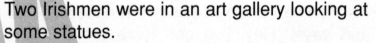

Two Irishmen were in an art gallery looking at some statues.

'See that statue over there?' said one. 'It's 1000 years and 12 weeks old.'

His friend was impressed.

'Wow, that's amazing! How did you know that is the exact date?'

'Because,' he replied, 'when I came here 12 weeks ago, one of the guides told me it was 1000 years old.'

Did you hear the one about the Irish water polo team?

All their horses drowned!

'Do you know the difference between a Dublin wedding and a Dublin funeral?' an Irishman asked.

'No, I don't,' replied his friend.

'One less drunk.'

An Irishman is up at the bar in a Belfast pub and says, 'Hey, I've got some great Paddy Scotsman jokes.'

The barman's such a big fella he makes Desperate Dan look like a nine stone weakling.

'Look, before you start, I'm warning you, I'm Scottish.'

'Oh, no problem,' says the Irishman. 'I'll tell them very slowly.'

An American in need of a toilet was hurrying through a dockyard when he stopped O'Malley, an Irish docker, man and boy.

'Howdy partner,' the Yank drawled, 'do you know where the urinal is?'

O'Malley looked around and then said, 'No idea Sir. How many funnels does it have?'

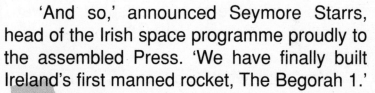

'And so,' announced Seymore Starrs, head of the Irish space programme proudly to the assembled Press. 'We have finally built Ireland's first manned rocket, The Begorah 1.'

'And when will it be launched?' asked an eager journalist.

'As soon as we find a big enough bottle,' replied Seymore.

NEWSFLASH!

It has been reported that the Irish arm of the SAS secretly entered Iran recently. Unfortunately things didn't go to plan when the leader misheard his instructions and led a dawn raid on Tehran Zoo and successfully released 25 ostriches.

Two Irishmen were at an air display and were marvelling at the aerobatics the planes were performing.

'You know what?' said one. 'I wouldn't like to be up there in one of those things.'

'You know what?' replied his friend. 'I wouldn't like to be up there without one!'

'I was really close to winning the Lotto last week!' Liam said to Shaun.

'Really?' asked Shaun. 'How many numbers were you out?'

'Six,' said Liam.

Two Irishmen wanted to check that the indicators on their car were working. One of them went round the back to check.

'Yes they are, no they're not, yes they are, no they're not…' he called.

MEDICAL NEWS!
The Irish have just set up a new clinic for people who want to stop smoking. It's called Smokers Anonymous.

Any time you get the urge to light up a cigarette, you just ring them up and they send a man over and you get drunk together instead.

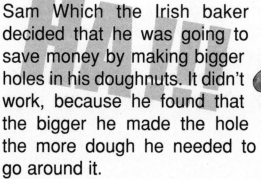

Sam Which the Irish baker decided that he was going to save money by making bigger holes in his doughnuts. It didn't work, because he found that the bigger he made the hole the more dough he needed to go around it.

'Mammy, can I have an ice cream?' asked a little Irish girl.

'No!' said her mum. 'It's too cold.'

The little Irish girl thought for a while and then said, 'Mammy, can I have an ice cream if I put my coat on?'

O'Shalley met O'Malley in the street and asked him why he was wearing a neck brace and had his arm in a sling.

'Oh, I had an accident when I was raking up some leaves,' groaned O'Malley.

'What happened?' asked O'Shalley.

'I fell out of the tree.'

'I'm afraid your pet chameleon is dead,' said Dr Downboy, the vet, to the Irishman. 'It appears to have died from exhaustion.'

The Irishman sighed. 'I knew I should have never put its cage next to those disco lights.'

An Irishwoman went to her solicitors Grabit, Haveit and Run, and said that she wanted a divorce from her husband.

'I see,' said Will Grabit. 'Do you have a grudge?'

'No,' said the Irishwoman. 'We only have a carport.'

An Irishman went into a café and asked if the owner would fill his flask up with coffee.

'Of course I can,' said the café owner. 'Give it to me.'

'Thank you,' smiled the Irishman, handing over the flask. 'I'll have six cups; two black, three white and one without sugar please.'

Did you hear the one about the Irish seasickness tablets?

They really work – you just take one with a glass of water and then you are seasick!

'Can you lend me a tenner?' Thaddy asked.

'Of course I can,' said Paddy, 'as soon as I get paid.'

'When will that be?' Thaddy enquired.

'As soon as I start working,' replied Paddy.

An American tourist walks into an old country pub in Tipperary.

'Hey man, what a quaint ol' Irish pub,' he says. 'It's got a real atmosphere and look, it's even got sawdust on the floor.'

The barman looks at him.

'That's not sawdust, that's last night's furniture.'

An Irishman was in the optician's picking up his new glasses.

'Right,' said the optician Dr Seymore Clearly, 'here's your new glasses. Now your eyesight isn't too bad, but you must wear them when you're working.'

'Oh,' said the Irishman, 'that might be a problem.'

'Why's that?' asked the optician.

'I'm a boxer,' replied the Irishman.

A little Irish girl was at the lounge table doing her geography homework while her Dad was watching the football on the television.

'Dad!' she called. 'Where are the Himalayas?'

Without looking away from the TV her dad said, 'I don't know. Ask your Mum, she puts most of the stuff away in this house.'

A little Irish girl came home from school looking very pleased with herself.

'Mammy, I won a prize today in nature studies.'

'That's nice,' said Mammy. 'How did you win?'

'Well, the teacher asked the class how many legs an emu has, and I said four.'

'Four?' questioned Mammy. 'But an emu has two legs.'

'I was the nearest,' smiled the little girl.

An Irish farmer was trying to raise chickens, but it just wasn't working.

'I just don't know what I'm doing wrong,' he said to his wife.

'Perhaps you're planting them too deep?' she replied.

A cook had just started working in an Indian restaurant in Dublin when he collapsed and the Manager had to call the paramedics.

'What happened?' asked the Irish paramedic.

'Well,' said the Manager, 'he was making a meal and sampling some of the ingredients, when he just passed out.'

'Which ingredients was he sampling?'

'Um, well... a bit of cumin, some turmeric and a couple of other spices,' replied the Manager.

The Irish paramedic sighed. 'Well, that explains it then.'

'Why, what's wrong with him?' demanded the Manager.

'He's in a korma,' he said.

It was very cold and an Irishman decided to go fishing. He started to dig a hole in the ice when he heard a big booming voice call:

'Do not cut a hole in the ice.'

The Irishman looked around but couldn't see anybody, so he finished the hole and started to fish in the ice. Then came the big booming voice again.

'Do not fish in the ice.'

The Irishman was confused as he couldn't see anybody, then he thought and said aloud,

'Is that you God talking to me?'

'No,' said the booming voice. 'It's the Manager of the ice rink.'

Did you hear the one about the Irish restaurant that said they served a 7-course Irish meal?

They gave you a potato and a six-pack of stout!

'What ya doing pardner?' called the American tourist when he saw an Irishman digging in his garden.

'I'm digging up me potatoes,' said the Irishman picking up a potato to show the American.

'Call that tiny thing a potato?!' drawled the American. 'Back home we have potatoes ten times the size of that.'

'Ah yes Sir,' said the Irishman, 'but we only grow ours to fit our mouths.'

The manager of a Dublin football team was giving a pep talk before the start of a big cup match.

'OK boys, we're in trouble today because everything in our favour is against us. The referee has just told me that it's getting foggy out there, so he might be playing extra time first. So what I think is this, we've got to equalise before they score to have a chance of winning the game.'

53

Paddy Englishman, Paddy Scotsman and Paddy Irishman had escaped from prison and were in a barn hiding in some sacks when the police came.

A policeman kicked the sack Paddy Englishman was in and Paddy Englishman went, 'Miaow.'

'Just a cat in that sack,' said the policeman. Then he kicked the second sack and Paddy Scotsman went, 'Quack, quack.'

'Just a duck in that one,' said the policeman.

It was going so well. Then the police kicked the last sack and Paddy Irishman went, 'Potatoes.'

'Has that Irish girl been using the computer to write letters again?' asked an angry Boss.

'Yes she has,' said one of her work colleagues.

'I thought so,' sighed the Boss. 'There's Tippex all over the screen again.'

An Irishman went into a pet shop and bought 99 budgerigars, tied them to himself, jumped off a cliff and plummeted to the ground. The next day he limped back to the pet shop, bought 99 chickens, tied them to a kite, took a painful running jump off the same cliff, and once again plummeted to the ground. The following day he returned to the pet shop on crutches and covered in bandages. He asked for 99 parrots.

'I hope you don't mind me asking?' said the pet shop owner. 'You've had 99 budgies and 99 chickens, why do you want 99 parrots?'

'Well,' said the Irishman. 'That budgie-jumping and hen-gliding were a waste of time so I thought I'd have a go at Parrotchuting.'

Did you hear the one about the Irish burglar?

He broke into a bookie's and lost twenty pounds!

Liam asked Shaun if he could borrow a file.

'What for?' Shaun asked.

'Well, my hamster has got a bit of hard skin on the top of its head and I want to file it off.'

'You can't do that,' said Shaun. 'You'll kill it!'

'No I won't,' replied Liam. 'I'll be gentle.' So Shaun gave Liam the file.

A couple of days later Liam returned the file.

'How did it go?' asked Shaun.

'Oh the hamster died.'

'I told you it would,' Shaun boasted. 'I told you not to use a file.'

'Oh it wasn't the file that killed him,' said Liam. 'I think I had him in the vice too tight.'

Did you hear about the Irish girl who asked her mammy for an encyclopaedia for Christmas?

Her mammy said 'No' and that she could walk to school like the rest of the kids.

An Englishman, a Scotsman and an Irishman go into a bar and they all order a Guinness. Suddenly a fly drops into the Englishman's drink. The Englishman sees the fly, stares at it for a few moments, then picks it up and throws it in the Scotsman's glass. The Scotsman sees the fly in the head of his Guinness, stares at it for a few seconds, shrugs his shoulders and drinks the beer. He spits the fly into the Irishman's pint. The Irishman sees the fly and quickly grabs it and starts to shake it saying, 'Spit it out! Spit it out!'

'Hey this e-bay is good,' said Pat. 'I've just sold my television for fifty pounds.'

'That's great,' said Paddy. 'What are you going to do with the money?'

'Well I've got enough money to buy a video recorder now.'

It was Molly Malone's first day working at the restaurant and the manager called her over.

'Molly, why has it taken you four hours to fill up four salt-cellars?'

'I'm sorry,' apologised Molly, 'but it's very difficult to get the salt into that little hole in the top of the lid.'

Mary and Colleen were finally coming home from the winebar and were staggering along.

'Colleen,' asked Mary looking up into the sky, 'is that the sun or the moon?'

'I don't know,' replied Colleen. 'I don't live around here.'

Did you hear the one about the Irishman who decided to enter the Dublin marathon?

He started to train very hard. For six weeks he ran 5 miles a day. The training was going well but at the end of the six weeks he was 210 miles away from the race!

An Irish girl went to her physician, Dr Ann Nurses, to complain about a strange pain she was experiencing.

'Doctor,' she said, 'every time I drink a cup of tea I get a sharp stabbing pain in my eye.'

'That sounds unusual,' replied the Doctor. 'Why don't you make a cup of tea now, so I can see what happens.'

So the Irish girl made a cup of tea and sure enough she got the sharp stabbing pain in her eye.

'Ah, I see the problem,' smiled the Doctor.

'What is it?' asked the Irish girl, concerned.

'Well, when you make another cup of tea, remember to take the spoon out before you drink it.'

Two Irish workmen were working on a building site.

'The boss says we're getting a thousand bricks delivered today,' said one.

'A thousand?' replied his friend. 'How many is that?'

'Oh millions...'

A man saw a sign in an Irish restaurant window that read, 'CHICKEN DINNER 50p'. Thinking this a bargain, he went in and ordered a chicken dinner for 50p. A few minutes later the Irish waiter returned and set down a plate of grain.

'What's this?' asked the surprised man.

'It's grain, Sir,' said the waiter.

'But I ordered a chicken dinner!' the man protested.

'Well,' sniffed the Irish waiter, 'it's what our chickens get for dinner.'

An Irish girl stood by the roadside while the vehicle breakdown man looked under the bonnet of her car.

'Ah, that's your problem,' he said after a few minutes of investigation. 'You've got a flat battery.'

'Oh,' said the Irish girl. 'What shape is it supposed to be?'

Two Irishmen had been stranded on a desert island for over three years when one day a boat washed up on to the beach.

'Quick, quick!' shouted one of the Irishmen excitedly. 'Look what I've found.'
His friend came running over and was delighted. 'At last!' he cried. 'We can leave the island and return home.'

So that night the two friends set about chopping up the boat to make a raft.

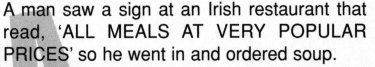

A man saw a sign at an Irish restaurant that read, 'ALL MEALS AT VERY POPULAR PRICES' so he went in and ordered soup.

When he finished his meal, the Irish restaurant manager gave him the bill and the man was shocked.

'£10 for a bowl of soup!' he exclaimed. 'I thought all your meals were at popular prices?'

'Well, I like them,' said the manager.

An Irishman went on 'Mastermind' and after 'Passing' when the Quiz-master asked him his name, he was given another question.

'How many 'D's are there in *Indiana Jones and The Last Crusade*?'

The Irishman thought for a while and then said '110.'

'110!' laughed the Quiz-master. 'How on earth did you work that out?'

'Easy,' said the Irishman as he counted on his fingers. 'De De De, Dee, Dah, Dah Daaa, De, De, De, Dee, Dah, De, Dah Dah Daah! De, De, De....'

Have you heard the one about the Irishman who sits out in the garden when it is sunny?

Just the merest hint of sunshine and he stops what he was doing and goes outside to relax in amongst the flowers and grass.

He's called Paddy O'Furniture!

Two Irishmen were discussing their forthcoming holiday.

'So where are you going?' asked the first Irishman.

'America,' said the second.

'Oh, where?'

'Hippopotamus,' replied the second Irishman.

'Where?'

'Hippopotamus,' replied the second Irishman. 'It's near Niagara Falls.'

'You mean Buffalo,' sighed the first Irishman.

'I knew it was some sort of big animal.'

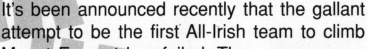

It's been announced recently that the gallant attempt to be the first All-Irish team to climb Mount Everest has failed. The courageous team led by Irish Mountaineering expert, Cliff Face, tried very hard and would have made it to the summit, but they ran out of scaffolding.

There was a power cut in the Delaney household just as the doctor was about to deliver Mrs Delaney's baby.

'What shall I do Doctor?' asked nervous Mr Delaney.

The doctor told Delaney to go and get a lantern and hold it up so that the doctor could see what he was doing, which is what Mr Delaney did.

Soon the baby arrived. Mr Delaney was about to put the lantern down when the doctor said, 'wait a minute, hold the lantern up.'

Mr Delaney did as he was told and a few minutes later there was another baby. Then there was another and another.

'Doctor,' asked Mr Delaney, 'do you think it's the light that's attracting them?'

Did you hear about the Irishwoman who wanted an animal skin coat for her birthday?

Her husband bought her a donkey jacket!

'So how's the new diet going?' Shaun asked Liam when they met in the street.

'Oh it's brilliant,' replied Liam. 'It's a whiskey diet.'

'A whiskey diet?' said Shaun in surprised tones.

'Yeah, I have whiskey for breakfast, whiskey for lunch, whiskey for dinner and whiskey for supper.'

Shaun was impressed and asked, 'is it working?'

'Well I lost three days last week,' said Liam.

An old dishevelled three-legged Irish wolfhound limps into a saloon in the Old Wild West. He limps across the floor and drags himself up to the bar. The bartender looks at this sorry creature and asks what he wants.

The old dog replies in a husky voice, 'I'm looking for the man who shot my paw.'

An Irishman was up in court and as he stood in the dock, the Judge, who had no thumbs and was known as Justice Fingers, gave him a hard stare.

'Tell me, is this the first time that you've ever been up before me?'

The Irishman was confused and stared back at the Judge. 'I don't know your honour, what time do you generally get up?'

A man went in to an Irish newsagent and asked for a newspaper.

'Would you like today's or tomorrow's?' asked the newsagent.

'Erm, I'll have tomorrow's,' said the man.

'OK,' said the Irish newsagent. 'Come back in the morning.'

An Irishwoman was stopped by the police and was asked if she could show them her driving licence.

'I wish you people would make your minds up,' said the angry Irishwoman. 'Yesterday you took away my licence and today you want me to show it to you!'

🍀

Did you hear the one about the Irishman who was very happy when he sold his house?

His landlord sued him!

🍀

An Irishman is out for a stroll along the riverbank when he sees his friend, on the opposite bank.

'Hey!' he shouts. 'How can I get to the other side?'
His friend looks up and down the river and shouts back.

'Ah, don't worry about that, you're already on the other side."

'Is that Belfast double three, double three?' asked the voice when an Irishman answered the phone.

'No,' said the Irishman. 'This is Belfast 3333.'

'Oh, I'm so sorry to have bothered you,' said the voice.

'Not to worry,' said the Irishman. 'The phone was ringing anyway.'

An Irishman rang the maternity ward and said excitedly, 'I'm going to bring my wife in. She's going to have a baby.'

'Is this her first baby?' asked the nurse on the other end of the line.

'No!' said the Irishman. 'It's her husband.'

'I only boil my eggs for two minutes,' Colleen told Nolleen when she popped round for breakfast.

'Why only two minutes?' asked Nolleen.

'Well if I held them in any longer, the water would burn my hand.'

A weary hiker was walking past a farm in Galway when the farmer asked him if he would like to come in for something to eat. The hiker was very hungry and took the farmer up on his offer. Sitting in the farm kitchen enjoying a large bowl of soup, he was amused to see a pig scurrying around and sniffing at his legs.

'Your pig is a curious little chap,' said the hiker.

'Not really,' said the farmer. 'He's just hungry, and he's waiting for you to finish with his bowl.'

Two Irish builders were flying over the Sahara Desert. One of them looked out of the plane's window.

'Will you look at all that sand?'

'Aye,' replied his friend. 'I wonder when the cement is going to be delivered?'

Liam was looking very shocked when he came round to Shaun's house.

'What's the matter?' asked a concerned Shaun.

'I woke up this morning and an aeroplane crashed into the side of my house.'

'That's awful!' Shaun gasped. 'What happened?'

'It's OK, no one was hurt but I must have left the landing light on.'

Farmer O'Malley kept two horses and had great difficulty telling them apart.

He tried putting them in separate fields, but that didn't work.

He tried giving them different names, but that didn't work.

Finally he came up with a solution.
He measured them both and found out that the black one was bigger than the white one.

Two Irish farmers were leaning on a gate looking at a herd of cows in a field.

'I bet I can tell you how many cows there are in that field before you,' said the first farmer.

'You're on,' said the second farmer, and started counting.

He hadn't got far when the first farmer said, '100.'

'Wow,' said the second farmer, 'how did you do that so quickly?'

'Easy, really,' said the first farmer. 'I just counted all the legs and divided by four.'

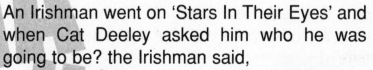

An Irishman went on 'Stars In Their Eyes' and when Cat Deeley asked him who he was going to be? the Irishman said,

'Tonight Cat, I'm going to be Glenn Miller.'
The studio audience applauded as the Irishman disappeared into the smoke... and was never seen again.

'My missus is never satisfied,' moaned an Irishman to his friend.

'Why's that?' asked the friend.

'Well, it was her birthday and I asked what she wanted and she said something with diamonds in it. So I got her something.'

'And didn't she like it?' said the friend.

'Nope!' sighed the Irishman. 'She threw the whole pack of playing cards back in my face.'

Brendan was standing in the hallway 'suited and booted' ready to go out, but his wife was still getting ready.

'Bridget!' he called. 'Will you hurry up woman, otherwise we'll be late and miss the film.'

'Oh hold yer whist, Brendan McDougall!' shouted back his wife. 'Haven't I been telling you for the last hour, that I'll be ready in a couple of minutes?'

A Welsh mum, a Scottish mum and an Irish mum were chatting while they were waiting for their children to come out of school.

'I called my little boy, David,' said the Welsh mum, 'because he was born on St David's Day.'

'Oh that's nice,' said the Scottish mum. 'In fact I called my little boy Andrew, because he was born on St Andrew's Day.'

'Well isn't that strange.' said the Irish mum. 'I did the same. Oh, here he comes now.' She waved at her little boy and said, 'Hello Pancake, how was school today?'

The foreman on the building site was surprised to see his Irish builder hopping along a plank of wood that stretched across two pieces of scaffolding.

'Oi,' called the foreman, 'why are you hopping?'

'I don't think this plank will take my full weight.'

A police officer stops two Irish drunks as they stagger out of the pub.

'OK lads,' says the policeman, 'what are your names and addresses?'
The first drunk says, 'My name is Michael Mulligan of no fixed address.'

'I see. And what about you?' the policeman asks the second drunk.

'Oh, I'm Dolan Dougan and I live in the flat above Michael.'

It was an Irishman's first day working at the sawmill when the manager saw him leaping about and clutching his hand.

'What's the matter?' he asked as he rushed over to help.

'I've lost me finger!' screamed the Irishman.

'How did you do that?' said the manager.

'Well,' said the Irishman, 'I just touched this big spinning thing here like thi... Ahh! There goes another one!'

An Irishman was driving home one night and had stopped at some traffic lights when a policeman on a bike pulled up beside him and tapped on the window.

'At last!' said the policeman breathlessly. 'I've been after you since that last roundabout.'

'What is it officer?' asked the Irishman.

'Did you know that your wife fell out of the car when you went round that roundabout?'

'Oh thank goodness for that,' sighed the Irishman. 'For a minute there, I thought I'd gone deaf.'

'Hello,' said the man who knocked on Mr O'Grady's door. 'I'm collecting for the local swimming baths.'

'Oh right,' said Mr O'Grady. 'Wait here.'
Off Mr O'Grady went into the house and came back a couple of minutes later with a bucket of water.

An Irishman was having terrible trouble running up and down a tall ladder with a tape measure.

'What're you doing?' asked his friend.

'The boss wants me to measure this ladder.'

'Well, why don't you lay it down and measure it?' suggested the friend.

'That'll be no good,' said the Irishman. 'He wants the height, not the length.'

An Irishman rang up his local newspaper and asked how much it would be to put a 'For Sale' advert in the paper.

'That's a pound an inch,' replied the person from the paper.

'Oh that's far too expensive,' said the Irishman. 'I've got a 12ft ladder to sell.'

The head of the Irish Football Association called a press conference to make an important announcement.

'Ladies and Gentlemen,' he began, 'I've called you all here today to announce that we have picked the team to represent Ireland in the next World Cup. It's Brazil.'

Did you hear about the Irish swimming baths?

They had to close lanes 3, 4 and 7 due to hot weather and a water shortage!

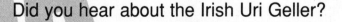

Did you hear about the Irish Uri Geller?

He could bend spoons, forks, knives, anything, completely in half just by rubbing them.
Unfortunately the other day he had a neckache and tried to rub it better, but his head fell off!

Did you hear the one about the Irishman who ran into his local DIY shop and covered himself in white, green and blue paint?

He was arrested and eventually taken to hospital, where the doctor said that he was suffering from emulsional distress!

An Irishman's neighbour caught him letting his dog foul the path right outside his gate.

'Oy!' shouted the angry neighbour. 'Why don't you train your dog to do that in the gutter?'

'I did,' said the Irishman, 'but he kept falling off the roof.'

An Irishman was walking down Dundalk High Street minding his own business when a man stopped him and asked, 'Excuse me, do you know if there is a B&Q in Dundalk?'
The Irishman thought for a while, and then a bit longer, and finally said, 'No, but there are two Ds and a K.'

A man was walking past a farm in Galway when he saw a farmer in a field with a three-legged pig.

'You don't see too many of those,' called the man.

'That pig, Sir,' said the farmer, 'is a hero. That pig woke me and my family up when the farmhouse caught alight last week and that pig led us to safety. When the fire brigade got lost, that pig, Sir, found them and led them here. And that pig then went back into the flames and rescued the cat, just getting out before the top floor fell through.'

'Is that how he lost his leg?' asked the man.

'Oh no Sir. When you've got a pig that is that brave and heroic, it seems a shame to eat him all at once.'

'This is Aer Lingus flight 5673 to control.'

'Come in Aer Lingus 5673, this is control.'

'Control, we are flying at a height of 21,000 feet. One of my stewards has reported a faulty fuselage door and is at this moment holding on to it.'

'OK Aer Lingus 5673, can you ask the steward to just let go of it for a second and see how far it moves?'

'Will do Control.'

'This is Control to Aer Lingus flight 5673. Has the steward let go of the door?'

'Yes he has, Control.'

'And how far did it move?'

'About 21,000 feet, Control.'

An Irishwoman wasn't that keen on having cable television, on account of the workman having to dig all those trenches. Her husband finally persuaded her to have it, by telling her that they could always get a new carpet when the workman had gone.

An Irish girl was working behind the counter at the Post Office when a man came in with a letter and asked for a first class stamp. The Irish girl gave the man the stamp and he asked, 'Do I put this on myself?'

'No ya big eejit,' said the Irish girl. 'Sure you stick it on the envelope.'

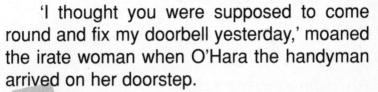

'I thought you were supposed to come round and fix my doorbell yesterday,' moaned the irate woman when O'Hara the handyman arrived on her doorstep.

'I did. I rang twice, but got no answer.'

Aer Lingus flight 2347 was just coming into Shannon Airport when the Controller called on the radio.

'Aer Lingus flight 2347, you have traffic at 3 o'clock, 7 miles out.'

'Could you help us out on that?' asked the pilot. 'We're all wearing digital watches.'

Two Irish hunters were looking at some tracks on the ground.

'I reckon those are deer tracks,' said the first Irishman.

'No, I think they are fox tracks,' replied his friend.

'Deer!' argued the first Irishman.

'Fox!' argued the other one back.

They were still arguing when the train ran them over.

An Irishman went up to the woman behind the counter and said in a loud voice, 'I'd like a pint of the black stuff and a packet of cheese and onion crisps, please.'

'Sir, this is a library!' said the woman, quietly.

'Oh sorry,' apologised the Irishman. Then he whispered, 'I'd like a pint of the black stuff and a packet of cheese and onion crisps, please.'

Boylan and Moylan were staggering home from the pub along a country road as black as the pints they had been drinking. Suddenly Boylan tripped over something.

'Are you OK, Boylan?' called Moylan.

'I'm fine,' slurred Boylan. 'But I think we're in a graveyard.'

'Why do you say that?' asked Moylan.

'Because I can see a stone here that says a man lived to 110!'

Moylan was amazed. '110! Was it anybody we knew?'

'I don't think so,' Boylan burped. 'His name was Miles from Galway.'

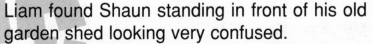

Liam found Shaun standing in front of his old garden shed looking very confused.

'What's wrong Shaun?' asked Liam.

'Oh I want to whitewash my garden shed,' replied Shaun, 'but I'm not sure what colour I want to do it in.'

There was an Irish restaurant that claimed it could serve any meal requested, so a man went in and asked a waiter for an Elephant and Tortoise sandwich.

The Irish waiter looked very embarrassed.

'Aha, you can't give me that can you?' said the smug man. 'I've caught you out haven't I?'

'You certainly have Sir,' said the Irish waiter. 'We've completely run out of bread.'

An Irishman went into his local barber shop and playground equipment suppliers called 'Short Back and Slides'. He asked the barber:

'Excuse me, I wonder if you can help me. My hair keeps falling out. Do you have anything for that?'

'Certainly Sir,' said the barber, giving the Irishman a paper bag. 'Here, keep it in this.'

An Irishwoman had a rare medical condition, but made an amazing recovery after an operation that involved replacing some of her brain cells with cells from pig's skin. The operation was a success, but there was an unusual side effect. Her hearing was no longer the best, especially her left ear. She got a lot of crackling in it.

An Irishwoman runs into a police station.

'Help me!' she screams. 'I just seen a man get in my car and steal it.'

'OK madam, calm down,' says the Desk Sergeant. 'Could you possibly describe the man?'

'No,' says the Irishwoman. 'But I did get the car registration number.'

Two Irishmen were playing Trivial Pursuit. One of them rolled the dice and it landed on Science & Nature.

'OK,' said his friend, 'here's your question. If you are in a vacuum and someone calls your name, will you be able to hear it?'

The Irishman thought for a while and then asked, 'is it on or off?'

'They're a couple of fine looking animals,' commented a man when he saw an Irishman taking his dogs for a walk.

'Thanks,' said the Irishman. 'The black one is called Rolex and the brown one is called Timex.'

'Unusual names for dogs,' the man said.

'Not really,' said the Irishman, 'they are watch dogs.'

Paddy went round to Thaddy's and saw him in the living room just staring at a pile of wooden doors, shelves, brackets and screws.

'What's up, Thaddy?' asked Paddy.

'Oh it's this self-assembly furniture I've just bought. It's rubbish,' moaned Thaddy. 'I've been watching it for three hours now and it still hasn't done a thing. If I have to wait any longer, I'm going to do it myself.'

An Irishman was doing 90mph down a motorway when the police stopped him. The Irishman said he was going so fast because he had diarrhoea and he wanted to get home before it was too late.

The police let him off, but warned him it was a very dangerous thing to do, even more dangerous if he had been driving a car at the time.

An Irishman was about to get on a bus with his pet monkey.

'Hey!' said the conductor. 'You can't bring that thing on my bus.'

'Why not?' asked the Irishman.

'I'm talking to the monkey.'

Another Irishman was about to get on a bus with his pet crocodile.

'Hey,' said the conductor, 'you can't bring a crocodile on my bus. What're you doing with it? You should take it to the zoo.'

'I did!' said the Irishman, 'and today I'm taking him to the cinema.'

Dylan the village drunk, when to his doctor, Dr D. Kat. After a thorough examination the doctor said, 'I've had a good look at you. I know it's the drink, but I can't really say what is wrong with you.'

'Sure, that's all right, Doc,' said Dylan. 'Shall I come back when you're sober?'

An Irishman was looking very pleased with himself.

'So why are you looking so pleased with yourself?' asked his friend.

'Well,' said the Irishman, 'I made my wife's eyes light up last night.'

'Really?' replied his friend. 'What did you do? Buy her a present? Take her out for a meal?'

'Nope,' smiled the Irishman. 'I shone a torch up her nose.'

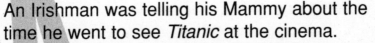

An Irishman was telling his Mammy about the time he went to see *Titanic* at the cinema.

'It was a great film,' said the Irishman, 'but I had to stay in the cinema for ages after the film ended.'

'Why was that?' asked his Mammy.

'They were only letting women and children out first.'

The Limerick Hotspurs Rover's goalkeeper let in 28 goals in one match. He trudged off the field feeling so dejected and with a nasty backache from all that bending over and picking the ball out of the back of the net. He slunk into the changing room, where all his teammates completely ignored him. He was so upset and distraught that he put his head in his hands to cry... and missed.

An Irishman was just about to leave the house, when his wife noticed he was only wearing one glove.

'Darling,' she called, 'why are you only wearing one glove?'

'Because,' the Irishman replied, 'the weather man on the telly said that it might be cold today, but on the other hand it could be warm.'

An Irishman was showing his friend his new smart business cards.

'Very nice,' said his friend.

'Thanks.'

'Just one thing,' his friend added. 'Why have you had your named printed on the front and the back of the card?'

'Ah that's in case,' said the Irishman, 'I give one to someone and they lose it.'

'Doctor, I'm worried about my wife,' the Irishman said. 'She's convinced that she's a bird.'

'That is very worrying,' said the Doctor. 'Tell you what, bring her in and I'll have a look at her.'

'I can't do that,' replied the Irishman.

'Why not?' asked the Doctor.

'She's just flown south for the winter.'

A judge rings up an Irish lawyer.

'How much would you charge me to answer three questions?'

'£1000, your honour,' replied the Irish lawyer.

'£1000!' exclaims the judge. 'That's very expensive, isn't it?'

'To be sure it is your honour,' answered the lawyer. 'And what's your last question?'

An Irishwoman went to see her doctor.

'It's my son, doctor,' she said. 'He keeps making mud pies and eating them.'

'There's nothing to worry about,' said the doctor. 'He'll grow out of it.'

'I hope so, Doctor,' said the Irishwoman, 'because his wife is getting very upset about it!'

Did you hear about Ireland's worst shepherd?

He used to call his sheepdog by putting his fingers in his mouth and shouting 'Rover!'

How did Ireland's worst shepherd count his flock?

'One sheep, Two sheep, Three sheep, another one, another one and another one and...'

An Irishman went into his bank for an appointment with his Bank Manager. He was invited into the Manager's office and got straight to the point.

'I was wondering Sir, how do I stand for a £500,000 bank loan?'

The Manager looked at the Irishman and said, 'On your knees.'

Sir Dinsmore Kildare, that famous Irish theatre actor was looking for lodgings in Belfast where he was about to appear in a play. He went up to one B&B, knocked on the door. The landlady appeared.

'Ah my good woman, I am seeking some accommodation in this fine city, whilst I perform for the lovely people within. This abode does indeed seem the ideal venue for one to rest before, and after, giving ones self in the name of ones art. Tell me pretty maiden, do you perchance have any low terms for actors such as I.'

'Certainly!' said the landlady. 'Clear off you pompous old eejit. Will that do?'

It was Christmas Eve in one particular Irish household and the husband was arguing with his wife.

'It's the same every year!' he bellowed. 'You're never satisfied. I buy the turkey, I pluck the turkey and I stuff the turkey. All you've got to do, woman, is kill it!'

An Irishman pulls up at a garage in his vintage car and fills it up with petrol. While he's paying the cashier says, 'that's an old car you got there.'

'You're telling me,' says the Irishman. 'It's the only car I know that's insured against fire, theft and Viking raids.'

'Wow!' says the cashier.

'That's nothing,' says the Irishman. 'I took the radiator out and found the original fireplace behind it.'

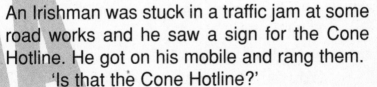

An Irishman was stuck in a traffic jam at some road works and he saw a sign for the Cone Hotline. He got on his mobile and rang them.

'Is that the Cone Hotline?'

'Yes it is,' said the lady on the other end. 'How can I help you?'

'I'd like a '99 with crushed nuts and raspberry sauce please,' said the Irishman.

Nola O'Nolan takes her car into a local garage to have some dents removed. The mechanic knows to look at her that she isn't the brightest woman in Ireland, and it's nearly 5:30 on a Friday afternoon.

'You don't need me to take those dents out. Just take the car home and then blow up the exhaust pipe and the metal will pop back into place.'

Nola thanks the mechanic and takes the car home.

Nolan O'Nolan, her husband, hears a huffing and puffing sound from behind the car. He opens the kitchen window and shouts, 'Nola, what on earth are you doing?'

Nola tells him what the mechanic had told her to do.

'You stupid woman,' says Nolan. 'It won't work with the windows down!'

A tourist was driving through the Irish countryside when his car broke down. When he was looking under the bonnet to see what was wrong, he heard a voice say, 'Your clutch is gone.'

The tourist looked around and all he could see was an old horse in a nearby field standing at a gate. The horse looked at him and said in a thick Irish accent, 'I'm telling ya, it's the clutch.'

The tourist nearly died with fright, and ran into the nearest pub and ordered a large drink and told the barman what the horse had said to him.

'Oh don't take no notice of him,' said the barman, 'he knows nothing about cars.'

An Irish couple were having an argument and the husband said, 'Do you know, I was a complete eejit, when I married you?'

'That's right, replied his wife, 'but I was in love at the time and didn't notice!'

Moylan was fishing by the river when Boylan came up to him.

'Caught anything yet?'

'Nothing,' replied a disappointed Moylan.

'What are you using for bait?' asked Boylan.

Moylan lifted his line out of the water and showed Boylan.

'Worms.'

Boylan took the worm off the hook, dipped it in his flask of Irish whiskey and handed it back to a puzzled looking Moylan.

'Try that?'

Moylan cast his line out and as soon as the worm hit the water, there was a great amount of splashing. His rod bent over and the line reeled out at an alarming rate.

'Have you got a bite?' asked Boylan.

'No,' shouted a struggling Moylan, 'but the worm's got a fish by the throat.'

A visitor was walking past an Irish farm when he saw the farmer lifting a pig up to an apple tree and holding it while it ate the apples off the branch.

'Excuse me,' said the visitor. 'If you just shook the tree so that apples fell to the ground, wouldn't it save time?'

'Doesn't matter, really,' said the Irish farmer. 'The pig's got plenty of time.'

An Irishman and his Swiss mountain guide, Toby le Rone, were caught in an avalanche. Thankfully they weren't hurt but they were firmly stuck in the snow. After a few hours a Saint Bernard came striding through the snow with a barrel of brandy tied under his chin.

'At last!' shouted Toby. 'Here comes man's best friend.'

'Aye,' said the Irishman, 'and would you look at the size of the dog bringing it.'

99

A spy was dropped into an Irish village with instructions to meet up with a contact by the name of Flynn. He was told that the recognition code to use was, 'It looks like rain.'

The first man he met was a farmer–he asked where he could find Mr Flynn.

'Now, Sir,' said the farmer, 'which Mr Flynn would that be, as we have a number of Flynns in this village? We have Father Flynn, Dr Flynn, Judge Flynn, Flynn the Undertaker, Flynn the Postman, Flynn the Chemist, Flynn the Mechanic, Flynn the Vet... In fact I'm a Flynn too. I'm Farmer Flynn.'

The spy had an idea and said, 'it looks like rain.'

'Ah,' smiled the farmer, 'you'll be wanting Flynn the spy.'

Did you hear the one about the Irishman who was sacked from his job at the 'M&M' sweet factory?

They sacked him for throwing all the Ws away!

Police found a skeleton in a cupboard when they raided a house in Cork. After further investigations and detailed forensic tests, it was revealed that they had found the skeleton of Malley O'Scalley, Ireland's Hide and Seek World Champion from 1901.

Did you hear the one about the Irish girl who wanted to buy a special pet?

She asked the local petshop for a wasp and the shopkeeper said:
    'I'm sorry Miss. We don't sell wasps.'
    'But you've got one in the window!'

Two Irishmen were sitting on the bus when one of them asked, 'Why do you have a see-through lunch box?'
    'So when I'm sitting on the bus,' came the reply, 'I know whether I'm going to work or coming home.'

Two bird spotters, Bill and Ben were out at night looking for owls. It wasn't long before they heard the familiar hoots.

'Listen!' said Bill. 'Hear that…?'

Ben listened and heard, 'Twit Too Who.'

'That's a Barn Owl,' said Bill.

Just then they both heard a 'Whoo, Whoo.'

'And that's a Tawny Owl.'

It went quiet for a while then they both heard another call. 'That's an Irish Owl,' said Bill.

'How do you know?' asked Ben.

'Listen,' said Bill, and the Owl went, 'What? What?'

Bernie and Bernadette spent Christmas in America and decided to go to a drive-in movie. They found one and parked. After waiting for nearly 5 hours for the movie to start Bernie was concerned.

'Are you sure there's a film on tonight?'

'Yes,' said Bernadette. 'There's a big sign back there advertising it.'

'What's it called?' asked Bernie.

'*Closed for the Winter.*'

An Irishman rang 999 in a panic.

'Can you help me?! My brother is lying on the floor unconscious.'

'What happened?' asked the operator.

'We were changing a light bulb...' the Irishman began.

'And did he receive an electric shock?' interrupted the operator.

'No, we were...'

'Did he fall off the ladder?' the operator interrupted again.

'No,' the Irishman said. 'In fact he wasn't up the ladder—I was. He was holding the ladder.'

'Well, how did he fall unconscious?'

'I think,' explained the Irishman, 'that he got dizzy spinning the ladder around for me, fell over and hit his head on the floor.'

Did you hear the one about the Irishman who climbed the chain link fence?

He wanted to see what was on the other side!

A man is on 'Who wants to be a Millionaire' and is on the £500,000 question when Chris Tarrant asks him:

'What animal lives in a sett? Is it;

A: A Rabbit

B: A Cuckoo

C: A Sheep

or

D: A Badger?'

The man is not sure, so he goes 50/50. He's left with 'B: A Cuckoo' and 'D: A Badger.'

He decides to 'phone a friend,' an Irish friend. So, his Irish friend answers the phone and after hearing the question, very confidently says, 'D: A Badger.' The man asks if he's sure and the Irishman remains very confident. Sure enough, it's right, and the man wins! He walks away with half a million pounds.

The next day the two friends meet up for a celebratory drink.

'Hey, how come you were so sure of that answer last night. I had no idea.'

The Irishman said; 'Sure it was easy – everyone knows that a cuckoo lives in a clock.'

'Well I think that was a successful trip,' said Captain Ahab O' Toole to a nearby sailor. 'We've been to Italy, Egypt, Turkey, Greece, Spain, Tunisia, Cyprus and Malta, all in eight days. I'd like to think that our passengers are more than satisfied with that, don't you think?'

'I don't think so, Captain,' replied the sailor.

'Why ever not?' asked the Captain.

'This is the Liverpool to Dublin ferry.'

Two Irishmen were walking down a road when a lorry passed them carrying a load of rolled up turf.

'Now,' said one of them pointing to the lorry. 'That's what I would do if I had the money.'

'What's that?' asked the second.

'Send my lawn away to be cut.'

A local Galway man was taking a stroll one Sunday afternoon when he came across a man in his skydiving suit hanging from a tree.

'What happened to you?' asked the Galway man.

'I was sky diving,' said the man, 'and my parachute failed to open.'

'You're not from round here, are you?' asked the Galway man.

'No,' replied the sky diver. 'What's that got to do with it?'

'Well if you were a local man, you would know that round here, nothing opens on a Sunday.'

A young Irish couple cuddled together one night after a romantic dinner and the boy said,

'I love you so much. I want to tell you everything that is in my heart.'

'Oh,' said the girl, 'that's so sweet, but just tell me everything that's in your head...It'll be quicker.'

An Irish girl got a call from her mammy who had just moved into a new modern house.

'How is it Mammy?'

'Oh it's very nice,' said her mammy, 'but I don't like the new washing machine.'

'Why not?' asked the girl.

'Well I put 6 of your father's shirts into it, pulled the chain and never saw them again.'

An Irishman wanted to take the car ferry. When he arrived at the terminal he saw the ferry about ten feet away from dock. Not wanting to miss it, he put his foot down and launched his car off the dockside. The car flew through the air, landing perfectly in a parking space on the ferry.

'How's that for a bit of driving,' said the proud Irishman to a nearby deckhand.

'It was great!' said the deckhand. 'But why didn't you wait? We were just about to dock.'

An Englishman, a Scotsman and an Irishman stood before a firing squad. The Captain of the squad shouted 'Ready... Aim...'

Suddenly the Englishman shouted, 'Earthquake!' The firing squad and the Captain were startled and as they looked around the Englishman escaped.

The Captain lined up the squad again and shouted 'Ready... Aim...'

Suddenly the Scotsman shouted, 'Tornado!' Once again the firing squad and the Captain were startled. When they looked back, the Scotsman had already run away.

With only the Irishman left, the Captain lined up the squad once again and shouted, 'Ready... Aim...'

The Irishman shouts, 'Fire!'

Two Irishmen were having a beer in the pub and chatting amiably.

'If you had a choice,' asked one, 'and you could have a conversation with anyone, living or dead, who would it be?'

'The living one,' the other Irishman replied quickly.

It was Halloween and an Irish chip shop owner was admitted to hospital with third degree burns all over his face.

'What happened to you?' asked the Doctor.

'I was bobbing for chips,' he replied.

An Irishman went round to see his Mammy for a cup of tea. As his Mammy prepared the cups and kettle, the Irishman couldn't help noticing that every time his Mammy tip-toed past the medicine cabinet and kept very quiet.

'Mammy?' asked the Irishman. 'Why do you creep past that medicine cabinet?'

'I don't want to wake up the sleeping pills in there.'

How do you keep an Irishman in suspense for hours?

Put him in front of a mirror and tell him to wait for the other person to say, 'Hello.'

An Irishman walks into a pub. The place is dead. No pool table, no dartboard, nothing, apart from a very pretty barmaid.

'What do you do for fun around here?' the Irishman asks the barman.

'I'll show you mate.'

The barman picks up a baseball bat and goes over to the corner of the pub where a gorilla is sitting and hits him over the head with the bat. The gorilla goes crazy. It jumps all over that place, smashing tables and glasses, finally leaping over the bar to give the pretty barmaid a kiss.

'That's amazing!' says the Irishman. 'Especially when he kisses the barmaid.'

'Do you want a go?' asks the barman patting the bat.

'OK,' says the Irishman. 'But just don't hit me as hard.'

'How are the new false teeth?' one Irishwoman asked of another.

'Oh, they're not bad,' the other sighed, 'but I'm leaving them out until I get used to them.'

An Irishwoman went into a fish and chip shop and asked for some fish and chips.

'Certainly,' said the man behind the counter, 'it won't be long.'

'Well make sure it's a fat one then,' said the Irishwoman.

An Irishman went into his local bank.

'I'd like to speak to the person who arranges loans, please.'

'Sorry Sir, but the loan arranger isn't here,' replied the cashier.

'OK then,' he replied. 'I'll have a word with Tonto.'

Did you hear the one about the vain Irishwoman who had too much plastic surgery?

She sat by her turf fire... and melted!

A rich Irish businessman was talking to a reporter.

'When I came to Dublin from Cork,' he began, 'all I had were the clothes I stood up in, a pair of shoes with holes in them and the laces missing, and a stick over my shoulder with a bundle made out of an old used handkerchief hanging from the end of it. But soon I owned half the city. I also owned half the office blocks, three cinemas, twelve night clubs, at least thirty building sites, a film company, a taxi company and a collection of high quality restaurants.'

'That's amazing,' said the reporter. 'It just shows what hard work can do. Just one last question: what did you have in the bundle on the stick?'

'Oh, about 60 million Euro,' replied the businessman.

It's a very well known fact that the English invented the toilet seat in 1643.
And very proud of it they were.
Then in 1645, the Irish added the hole.

An Irish girl was taking her driving test and had stalled the car.

'Now don't worry about that,' said the driving instructor.

'I'm sorry,' said the girl. 'I panicked.'

'It's OK; you're nervous,' the instructor said in calming tones.

'I didn't see the signs.' The Irish girl was very upset.

'No problem,' said the instructor. 'Just start the engine. Put the car in to first gear; indicate; check mirror and off we go.'

The Irish girl did as she was told. 'Which way shall we go?'

The instructor looked around. 'Well, if we go down this aisle, turn left at the meat counter, through the ten items only checkout and out the automatic doors we should get back to the car park.'

AIRLINE ANNOUNCEMENTS

'The British Airways flight to New York will be leaving at eighteen-fifty-five. Thank you.'

'The Qantas flight to Sydney will be leaving at nineteen-oh-five. Thank you.'

'The Air France flight to Paris will be leaving at nineteen-forty. Thank you.'

'The Aer Lingus flight to Dublin will be leaving when the big hand is on the twelve and the little hand is on the eight. Thank you.'

Famous Irish jockey G.G. Ryder was leading the field during a race at Leopardstown when suddenly he got hit on the head with a frozen turkey and a box of Christmas crackers. He managed to keep on riding, then he was hit with a dozen mince pies and a Christmas pudding until he was finally knocked off his horse by a well-aimed jar of cranberry sauce. At the end of the race, he complained to the stewards that he had been seriously hampered!

An Irishman went to the doctors with blisters all over his lips.

The doctor began his examination. 'That looks nasty. So, tell me how did you get those blisters on your lips?'

'Oh doctor,' said the Irishman. 'It always seems to happen after I've tried to blow out the light bulbs.'

Two Irishmen were running for the number 24, but just missed it.

'Oh Bejabers!' said the first Irishman. 'How are we going to get home now?'

'I know!' said the second Irishman. 'We'll wait for the number 12, and take it twice.'

Did you hear the one about the Irishman who threw away his brand new set of water skis?

He couldn't find a river that sloped!

An Irishman was filling up a bucket with fish from a private river.

'Right, caught you red-handed,' said the gamekeeper. 'Poaching fish from private property.'

'I'm not poaching,' said the Irishman.

'Don't try and talk your way out of this. You've a got a bucket of fish there.'

The Irishman looked in the bucket. 'Oh these aren't poached. They're my pet fish from my pond at home and I often bring them up here for a swim, then we go back home.'

'I don't believe you,' said the gamekeeper. So the Irishman emptied the bucket into the river and the fish swam away. After about an hour no fish had returned.

The gamekeeper finally laughed. 'See, I knew you were lying. Where are your fish now?'

'What fish?' said the Irishman.

The English Captain of a Royal Navy ship received a radio call from Paddy.

'Please alter your course 43 degrees to the West to avoid a collision.'
The Captain replied. 'Suggest *you* change your course to 43 degrees East to avoid a collision.'

'Ah now, I can't be doing that,' said Paddy calmly. 'So please alter your course 43 degrees to the West to avoid a collision.'

'I am the Captain of a Royal Naval Aircraft carrier and I say alter your course.'

'And I say again,' replied Paddy, 'You should steer her over a bit.'
The Captain was furious. 'Good God man, I am the Captain of Britain's biggest aircraft carrier with enough firepower to blast you out of the water. Who on earth are you?'

'I'm Paddy.'

'Paddy who?' shouted the Captain.

'Paddy the lighthouse keeper. Please alter your course.'

An Irishman was up in court in front of the judge for not paying maintenance money to his ex-wife. The judge, as a punishment decided to increase the Irishman's payments.

'Mr Finnegan I have decided to increase this allowance and give your ex-wife 75 pounds a week.'

The Irishman smiled.

'Thank you M'lud. You are a gentleman. I tell you what, I might even send her a bob or two myself.'

Colleen met a very sad Nolleen coming out of the vet's.

'What's the matter?' Colleen asked.

'The vet has just told me that I have killed my new Toy Poodle,' said Nolleen tearfully.

'What did you do?' questioned Colleen.

'Nothing much, I just tried to put new batteries into it,' Nolleen sobbed.

An Irishman was in his local pub supping his pint of stout when his wife burst in.

'I thought I'd find you here!' she shouted. 'You spend more time in this pub than you do at home with me. Why do you come here so much and...'

She takes a sip of his stout.

'Urgh! And drink this awful stuff?'

'And you thought I was out enjoying myself,' replied the Irishman.

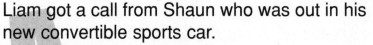

Liam got a call from Shaun who was out in his new convertible sports car.

'What's up?' asked Liam.

'I've locked my keys in the car,' said Shaun.

'Oh don't worry,' said Liam. 'I'll just get a clothes hanger and we'll try to get in that way.'

'That's great,' said Shaun, 'but would you hurry up? It looks like rain and I've got the top down.'

An Irishman applied for a job as a handyman in a Dublin hotel. The manager conducted the interview:

'So, can you do electrical work?'

'Er, no,' said the Irishman.

'Oh, what about plumbing?'

'Sorry, Sir, I can't do that either.'

'Right, what about carpentry?'

'Ah now, that's something with wood, isn't it? I can't do that either.'

'You can't do electrical work, can't do plumbing, or carpentry! Why did you apply for the job?'

'But I'm handy – I only live next door.'

An Irishman went into a fishmonger's.

'I'd like a pair of kippers for the wife, please.'

'I'm sorry, Sir,' said the fishmonger, 'we haven't got a pair left.'

'Oh, just give me two odd ones,' said the Irishman. 'She'll never notice.'

Three friends, an Englishman, an American and an Irishman went to a local Beer Festival. They went to the busy World beer tent and ordered their drinks.

'I'd like the best beer in the world,' said the American. 'Give me a Budweiser.'

The Englishman was next.

'Actually, I would like the best beer in the world, please. Please may I have a pint of English Best Bitter?'

'And what would you like?' the barman asked the Irishman.

'I'd like orange juice, please.'

The American and Englishman are shocked.

'Why aren't you having a Guinness?'

'Well, I thought, if you weren't drinking, then I wouldn't either.'

Did you hear about the Irish boy who ate all the Christmas decorations off the tree?

He's OK now, but he was rushed to hospital with Tinselitus!

A gorilla walks into a Belfast pub and asks for a pint of best.

'Certainly Sir,' says the Barman but as it's a gorilla, he decides to over-charge him.

'That'll be five pounds please.'

The gorilla opens his wallet and hands over a five-pound note.

The barman takes the money.

'I hope you don't mind me saying, but we don't get a lot of talking gorillas in Belfast.'

'At five pounds a pint, I'm not surprised!'

A man went to his local pet shop to return a cat he had bought a few weeks ago.

'When I bought that cat from you,' he said to the Irish pet shop owner, 'you said it was good for mice. Well let me tell you, this cat doesn't catch mice.'

'Well,' said the Irish pet shop owner. 'That's good for the mice then, isn't it?'

Thaddy went round to see Paddy and saw him lying on the floor in a pool of sweat in the middle of a freshly painted room. He noticed that Paddy was wearing a donkey jacket, under a woollen top and hood.

'Are you OK?' asks Thaddy.

'Oh I'm fine,' says Paddy, 'just doing some painting. It got a bit hot and I think I passed out.'

'I'm not surprised,' said Thaddy. 'Why are you wearing that jacket and woollen top?'

'Just following directions,' said Paddy, showing Thaddy the instructions on the paint tin. 'For best results, put on two coats.'

Did you hear the one about the little Irish boy who went to the cinema?

The girl on the ticket counter said that he couldn't get in because the film was an 18 and over only. He spent the rest of the afternoon finding 17 more friends to go with him.

A stranger walks into a Cork pub.

'I will give anyone here £100 if they can drink ten pints of stout in ten minutes.'

No one takes him up on the offer, but he does see Brophy leave the pub.

A little while later Brophy returns to the pub, and asks the stranger if the bet is still on. The stranger says it is, so Brophy takes the bet. Nine minutes later Brophy has drunk ten pints of stout.

'Well done,' says the stranger, handing over the hundred pounds. 'But tell me, where did you go when you left the pub earlier?'

'Oh,' said Brophy, 'I went down the road to the other pub to see if I could do it.'

Two Irishmen were walking past a cornfield. Out in the middle they saw another Irishman rowing a boat.

'Would ye look at that eejit,' said one of the Irishmen. 'It's people like that that give the Irish a bad name and makes everyone think we're stupid.'

'I know,' said his friend. 'And if I knew how to swim, I'd go out there and tip him out.'

Crash investigators were questioning the Irishman as he lay in a hospital bed after he had crashed his helicopter.

'So can you tell us what happened?' asked one of the officials.

'It's all a blur,' said the Irishman. 'All I can remember is that one minute I was flying along and was feeling a bit cold, so I decided to turn that big overhead fan off...'

An Irishman went into a pub and ordered a Martini. When it came, he took the olive out and put it in a small jar he was carrying. He then ordered another one and did the same thing with the olive. He kept doing this all evening until the jar was filled with olives, then staggered away from the bar. He was just about to leave when the barman called out to him.

'Excuse me. I couldn't help noticing what you were doing. What was that all about?'

'Oh nothing,' slurred the Irishman. 'The missus sent me out for a jar of olives.'

'Why are you late for work?' asked the Irish girl's boss.

'I'm sorry,' said the Irish girl, 'but I was using the escalator at the station. There was a power cut and I was stranded for nearly an hour.'

An Irishman returned home to see his brand new car in the living room.

'How on earth did that get there?' he screamed in horror.

'Easy,' his wife said. 'I just turned right at the kitchen.'

Did you hear the one about the shy Irish academic who went into the university library?

He took out a very big book out called *How to Hug*. When he got it back to his room he found out that it was volume seven of a set of encyclopaedias.

Did you hear the one about the Irish couple who went away for a camping weekend?

Unfortunately, they pitched their tent right in the middle of a cow field. That night the cows attacked them. It wasn't too serious; the boy got away with a few bruises, but the girl was badly grazed.

A stranger was surrounded by a gang of Irish boys, the leader of which gave him a dice and said,

'I want you to throw that dice and if it lands on 1,2 or 3, we're going to beat you up with our fists. But if it lands on 4 or 5 we're gong to beat you up with our boots.'

'W...W...What if I throw a six?' stammered the stranger.

The leader smiled. 'Then you get another go.'

Lying on his back looking up at the millions and millions of stars that lit up the night sky like a scattering of diamonds on a velvet drape, the Irishman thought to himself, 'The stars, the stars, what is the stars?'
and then after a little while…

'I wonder who's nicked my tent?'

The police arrested O'Malley who was drunk on battery acid and O'Shalley who thought he was a firework. They put them both in a cell overnight. In the morning they charged O'Malley and let O'Shalley off.

Two Irish hippies were talking to each other at a rock concert.
The first hippie asks, 'Hey bro, what would you do if you saw a spaceman?'
And the second hippie said, 'To be sure, I'd park me car in it.'

Did you hear about the unlucky Irishman? It started off when he was born. He was an only child and still wasn't Daddy's favourite. In fact his Dad tried to claim the birth against his accident insurance.

He was got a letter from *Reader's Digest* telling him that he *hadn't* reached the final round of the draw.

He peeled a banana once and it was empty.

He bought a duck and it sank.

He had a swimming pool and it burnt down.

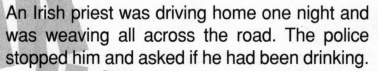

An Irish priest was driving home one night and was weaving all across the road. The police stopped him and asked if he had been drinking.

'Just from this bottle of water,' said the priest. The policeman took the bottle and sniffed it.

'This isn't water,' he said, 'it's wine.'

'It's a miracle!' exclaimed the priest.

'I've just received a fax from our Irish branch,' said the secretary to her boss.
The boss examined the fax.

'How do you know it's from our Irish branch? There's no address on it.'

'I know,' said the secretary, 'but it does have a stamp on it.'

An Irishman had drunk far too much and was wandering about trying to find out where he lived. Finally he got fed up and hailed a taxi.

'Take me to 46 Sally Gardens,' he slurred as he collapsed into the back seat.
The taxi driver looked about.

'You drunken fool, you're outside 46 Sally Gardens!'

'Right!' said the Irishman. 'And the next time, don't drive so fast.'

Liam and Shaun are sitting in front of the television watching the ten o'clock news, which is showing an item about a man threatening to jump off the roof of an office block in Dublin. Liam says to Shaun, 'I bet you £25 that he jumps!'

'£25?' says Shaun. 'Make it £50 and you've got a bet.'

Liam agrees and they shake hands on the bet and continue watching. Sure enough, the man jumps and lands on the firemen's safety sheet on the road below. Shaun takes £50 out of his wallet and hands it to Liam.

'I can't take your money, mate,' Liam says. 'I was cheating. I saw this on the six o'clock news, so I knew he was going to jump.'

'No, fair's fair,' says Shaun. 'That money is yours. In fact it was me who was cheating as I saw it on the five o'clock news, but I just didn't think he would do it again.'

Two Irishmen were discussing their childhood.

'When I was younger, I had two half brothers and a half sister,' one of the Irishmen reminisced. 'Then my Da took the chainsaw away from me.'

An Irishwoman had gone out for a drive in the brand new family car. After a while she rang her husband at home.

'Darling, I've got some news about the car. It's good news and then again it isn't.'

'What's the good news?' asked her husband nervously.

'The air bag works,' she shrilled.

Two IT experts were talking one day.

'Of course you know the difference between a computer and an Irishman?'

'No?' said his colleague.

'Well,' said the first IT expert, 'you only have to give the information to a computer once.'

Bob and Betty Dolley had a lovely holiday in Greece.

'They have lovely beaches,' Betty told her neighbour. 'Me and Bob had a great time burying each other in that soft golden sand.'

'Are you going again next year?' asked the neighbour.

'I think I might. I might even dig Bob up this time and bring him home with me.'

Mary couldn't help but notice that her friend had a black eye and a bandage wrapped around her head.

'Colleen, what happened to your face?'

'Oh,' said Colleen, 'I was putting some of that fancy toilette water on my face.'

'And?'

'Well, the lid fell down on my head.'

An Irishman returned home from the pub one night to a torrent of abuse from his wife.

'If you spent as much time at home, as you spend in that pub,' she moaned, 'I think I'd fall down dead.'

'There now,' said the Irishman, 'there'll be no use you trying to bribe me.'

Kerry and Terry were playing golf, when Kerry sliced his ball into the branches of a gigantic oak on one side of the green.

'Dat's unplayable,' said Terry. 'Dat's a penalty stroke.'

'No dat's alroight,' said Kerry. 'I think I can get dat. I got a tree iron in me bag.'

Sir Dinsmore Kildare the famous Irish theatre actor was directing his first stage play, but he wasn't very happy with an actor's death-bed scene.

'Dear boy!' he bellowed in theatrical tones. 'Could you please put some more life into your dying.'

An Irish steamroller driver came rushing into the bar shouting.

'Hey, can anyone tell me how tall a penguin is?'

'About two foot six,' said the Barman.

'Oh, begorah!' cried the Irishman. 'I've just run over a nun.'

A man walked into the pub with a small and cute puppy under his arm.

'What a nice looking dog!' said his Irish friend.

'Yeah,' smiled the man. 'I got it for the wife.'

'Seems like a fair swap,' replied the Irishman.

Now I'm not saying that she is the biggest woman in Ireland, but last week she bent over in Wexford and they had an eclipse in Kerry!

An Irishman presented his wife with a diamond ring for her birthday.

'Wow!' said his impressed wife. 'Is it a real diamond?'

'I hope so,' said the Irishman, 'otherwise that bloke in the pub has swindled me out of two pounds fifty.'

An Irishman was broken-hearted over his girlfriend. 'Why won't you marry me?' he asked as the tears ran down his face. Then he suddenly became suspicious. 'Is there someone else?'

'Oh, bejabers,' she sighed. 'There must be.'

Mick O'Mouse was a strange man on account of being born with two left feet. Most of the time it was fine, but when he went on holiday and he wanted something to wear on the beach, he spent hours in shoe shops looking for a pair of 'Flip-Flips'.

An Irish girl went in to see her Boss.

'Excuse me sir,' she said.

'What is it?' asked the Boss.

'You know that letter you asked me to write double-spaced?'

'Yes?'

'Well I was just wondering, do you want the photocopies double-spaced as well?'

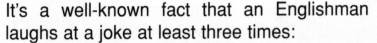

It's a well-known fact that an Englishman laughs at a joke at least three times:

Once when everybody he is with, gets it;

the second time a week later when he thinks he gets it;

and about a month later when an Irishman explains it to him.

Did you hear about the Irish woodworm?

It was found in a brick!

Two pilots were walking round a military airfield and one was pointing out all the different helicopters.

'See that one over there? That's an American Helicopter. You can tell by all the computers it has fitted on board.'

He then points to another one. 'And that one is a Russian Helicopter: the tell-tale sign is the type of missiles it has fitted.'

'What about that one over there?' the other pilot asked, pointing to another helicopter.

'Oh, that's an Irish Helicopter.'

'How do you know this time?' asked the second pilot.

'It's the only one fitted with an ejector seat.'

'Bridey, have you seen my new vest?' Dougal asked his wife.

'Oh yer big eejit, Dougal,' said Bridey. 'You're wearing it!'

'Oh thank God you noticed that,' said Dougal, 'otherwise I would have gone out without it.'

Two Irishmen were out shooting ducks. One of them took aim, fired, missed and hit a pigeon. The unfortunate bird fell from the sky and landed at their feet. One of them looked at the remains.

'Oh dear, you should have saved the bullet.'

'It's OK,' replied the other Irishman. 'The fall would have killed him anyway.'

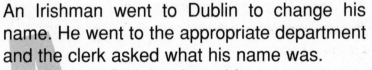

An Irishman went to Dublin to change his name. He went to the appropriate department and the clerk asked what his name was.

'Michael O'Hairy,' he said.

'I see,' said the clerk trying not to laugh. 'And what do you want it changed to?'

'Ernie.'

Two teams of Irish workmen were putting up telegraph poles. At the end of the day the site manager called the teams in.

'Well done lads,' he said. 'But I want to ask just one question to the foreman of the second team.'

'What's that Sir?' said the foreman of the second team.

'Well, I was just wondering why your team only put in two telegraph poles all day, when the other team did twenty?'

'Ah now, that was because they were cheating,' said the foreman. 'Did you see how much they left sticking out of the ground?'

Two Irish girls were talking about the new nightclub that had opened in town.

'I went there last night. It was packed to the roof. The dance floor was full, the bar was full—even the staircase was full. You can understand why nobody goes there.'

An Irishman arrived at Shannon Airport and wandered around the terminal in tears. Finally an airline official went up to him to ask what the matter was.

'I've lost all my luggage,' wept the Irishman.

'Oh dear,' said the official. 'What happened?'

'The cork fell out!' sobbed the Irishman.

A man was walking through a park when he saw two Irishmen digging. One was digging holes and the other one was busy filling them in again.

'Excuse me,' called the man. 'What are you doing?'

'Well,' said the Irishman digging the holes, 'there are generally three of us on this job. Me, Marley and Farley. I dig the holes, Marley puts the new trees in and Farley there fills in the holes. Marley has the flu.'

An Irishman had bought his first ever video player. He went to the video shop and in his excitement picked up the first video he saw and took it home. He put it in the player, settled down to watch the video. Unfortunately there was nothing but static on the screen and no matter how the Irishman played with the controls, he couldn't see a thing. He rang up the video shop and told them his problem.

'I'm sorry about that, Sir. Please bring it back and we shall exchange it.'

'Thanks,' said the Irishman and was about to put the phone down when the video shop clerk spoke.

'By the way, Sir, what's was the name of the video?'

The Irishman looked at the box, 'Head Cleaner.'

Irish scientists have discovered that we only use a quarter of our brain power.

They are still trying to discover what do we do with the other quarter!

Two Irishmen were flying home from a Drinks convention when the captain of the plane announced that one of the engines had failed, but that they had three left. Everything was all right, but the flight would take an hour longer.

A little while later the captain announced that another engine had failed, but that they had two left and that everything would be all right. The flight would now take two hours longer.

Not long after that the captain announced that a third engine had failed. Everything was all right, but the flight would now take four hours longer.

At this point one of them turned pale and said, 'I hope the last engine doesn't fail, otherwise we'll be up here all day.'

'Is that Interpol?' said the Irish voice on the phone.

'Oui,' replied the French officer.

'Can you send a bunch of roses to me Mammy?'

An Irishman went into an electrical shop in London and said to the assistant, 'I'd like to buy that television please.'

'I'm sorry,' said the assistant. 'Company policy: we're not allowed to serve Irishmen.'

Upset but not defeated, the Irishman went home, put on a wig, a false nose, some glasses and a suit and went back to shop and asked in an English accent.

'Here mate, I wanna buy that television, aw-right?'

'Look I'm sorry, but it's company policy: I'm not allowed to serve any Irishmen.'

'But how did you know I was Irish?' asked the Irishman disappointed.

'Because,' sneered the assistant, 'the television you want is a microwave.'

Not many people realise that an Irishman invented the first electric car. It went from Dublin to Belfast on only £10 worth of electricity. It never caught on though, because the extension lead cost over £25,000.

An Irishman was so desperate to get in to see the big match that he pushed in front of people waiting to get their tickets. A steward stopped him and told him to go to the back of the queue. Off the Irishman went but was back again very soon trying to push in.

'Oy!' said the steward. 'I thought I told you to go to the back of the queue.'

'I did,' said the Irishman, 'but there was already somebody there.'

Did you hear about the Irish Tooth Fairy?

She was sacked for leaving the tooth under the pillow and taking all the other teeth!

'I used to have a great variety act,' said Patrick O'Hattrick the retired Irish entertainer when he was being interviewed on TV.

'I had a parrot that could imitate famous film stars of the time. You name it, that parrot could imitate it. He could even walk like John Wayne and dance like Fred Astaire. Unfortunately though, we didn't get enough work. I was penniless and hungry so I had to eat him.'

'You had to eat your parrot?' said the shocked interviewer. 'What did it taste like?'

'Roast beef,' said Patrick. 'Like I said that parrot could imitate anything.'

Two priests were talking about Irish weddings.

'Of course you can always tell who the bride is when you're doing an Irish country wedding,' said one.

'How?' asked the second priest.

'She's the one wearing the white Wellington boots.'

It was Nola's birthday and Nolan was being a considerate husband.

'I'm going to get you a big—no a large—no an enormous—no a mega-enormous box of chocolates for your birthday,' he told Nola.

'But you know I'm on a diet!'

An Irishman came home from a hard day planting potatoes and talked to his wife.

'Just for a change, instead of just defrosting frozen food and putting in the microwave to cook, couldn't we have a traditional home-cooked meal?'

'Of course you can,' said his wife. 'I'll just open some tins.'

'You don't deserve a wife like me!' screamed the Irishwoman at her husband during a row.

'I don't deserve toothache either,' moaned the Irishman, 'but I've got it.'

Patrick became a monk and joined an order where he was only allowed to speak once every five years. At the end of the first five years the Abbot told Patrick that he could speak one sentence.

'The beds are very hard here,' he said.

Ten years later the Abbot allowed him another sentence.

'Can we do something about the beds, they're very uncomfortable?' asked Patrick.

Fifteen years later it was Patrick's time to speak again.

'You've still done nothing about the beds and my back is killing me.'

Twenty years later when the time came to speak Patrick stood up and said to the Abbot, 'Right! That's it! I'm leaving this order.'

'Good!' snapped the Abbot. 'You've done nothing but complain since you got here.'

'Nolan, do you think I'm getting crows' feet?' asked Nola as they prepared to go out for the evening.

'You might be,' said Nolan. 'Just keep your shoes on tonight and no one will notice.'

A dance instructor thought he could dance every dance there was. Then he heard about the 'Irish Butcher Dance.' Eager to learn this dance he travelled to Ireland to seek out the only 'Irish Butcher Dance' instructor, who told him that lessons would cost £750,000. So desperate was the dance instructor to learn it, that he sold his house, his car and most of his clothes to raise the money. He borrowed from the bank and loan sharks. He ate very little and never went out and finally had enough money. Handing the money over to the instructor, the now penniless man could hardly wait for his first lesson.

'OK, here we go,' said the Irish dance instructor. 'Butcher right foot in, Butcher right foot out, in, out, in, out, yer shake it all about.'

A boy asked his Irish girlfriend what she would like for St Valentine's Day.

'Do you like Chanel No 5?' he asked.

'Not really,' said the Irish girl, 'but there are some good programmes on ITV.'

The Irish Mountain Climbing team were in a spot of trouble, hanging off a cliff face holding onto a single rope.

'It's no good lads!' the leader shouted. 'There's ten of us holding on here and the rope won't hold—it'll snap. Someone has got to let go of the rope, so that nine of us will stand a chance of survival.'

Big Paddy shouted up from the bottom of the rope.

'I'll do it Boss. I'm the heaviest.'

'Thanks Paddy, and God be with you.'
Big Paddy let go of the rope and fell to his certain death.

'There goes a brave man,' said the leader. 'OK everyone: round of applause for Big Paddy.'

Miss O'Grundy was standing up in front of her class giving an English lesson.

'Now class,' she said, 'consider this sentence: "I didn't have no fun this weekend."'
'Who can tell me how I should correct this?'
Little Patrick put his hand up and said, 'Get a boyfriend, Miss.'

Farmer O'Toole had been invited round to supper by his neighbour, Farmer O'Giles. Knowing they both liked a drink or six, and that it would be dark on the walk home, O'Toole took a big stable lantern with him.

Sure enough, the farmers drank heartily and O'Toole set off home guided by his lantern.

The next day Farmer O'Giles rang.

'Did you get home alright last night?' he asked.

'Oh I did,' said O'Toole.

'Oh good,' said O'Giles, 'because you left your lantern here.'

'Did I?' asked puzzled O'Toole. 'But how did I get home?'

'I don't know,' replied O'Giles. 'Could I have my parrot and cage back please?'

Did you hear the one about the Irishman who was killed while drinking milk?

The cow fell on him!

Two Irish bird spotters were looking at something through their binoculars.

'And I say it's a magpie. It's got all the right markings and it's black and white.'

'It's not a magpie,' said the second spotter. 'It's a black-headed gull.'

'It's a magpie.'

'It's a black-headed gull.'

'It's a magpie.'

'It's a black-headed gull.' This went on for quite a while until another Irish bird spotter came up to ask what they were arguing about. They told him; so he had a look through his binoculars.

'You're both wrong,' he said. 'It's a Friesian cow.'

Two Irishmen were sitting on the bus when one of them asked, 'Why do you have a see-through lunch box?'

'So when I'm sitting on the bus,' came the reply, 'I know whether I'm going to work or coming home.'

The young Irish lad went round to his girlfriend's house to talk to her father about their plans.

'I'd like to ask you for your daughter's hand in marriage.'

The father thought for a moment.

'You'll take all of her, or nothing.'

An Irish teenager was standing on the corner having a sly cigarette when an elderly lady came up to him.

'Does your Mammy know you smoke?' she snapped.

The teenager took another puff, 'Does your husband know you speak to strange men?'

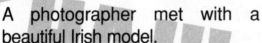

A photographer met with a beautiful Irish model.

'Would you mind if I photographed you in the nude?'

'Not at all,' she said. 'But won't you be cold? This studio is very draughty.'

'Is that O'Riley's Sign Writers?' shouted an angry voice down the phone.

'Yes it is,' answered O'Riley. 'How can I help you?'

'I'm Farmer McDonald and that eejit you sent round to paint the name of my farm has made a right mess of it. He's spelt "farm" wrong.'

'Oh dear,' said O'Riley. 'Did he put the "A" and the "R" round the wrong way?'

'No!' screamed the farmer. 'He spelt it E.I.E.I.O!'

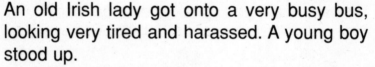

An old Irish lady got onto a very busy bus, looking very tired and harassed. A young boy stood up.

'You look tired. Would you like to sit in my seat for a while?'

'Oh no thank you,' she said. 'I'm in too much of a hurry to sit down.'

An Irish girl was chatting to another girl at a party.

'Hey, do you see that fella over there? He is so ugly! Looks like he fell out of the ugly tree and hit every branch on the way down. He'd make a good monster in a movie, and he wouldn't need any make up either.'

'Do you know who I am?' the girl asked.

'No,' said the Irish girl.

'I'm that fella's girlfriend.'

'Oh? Do you know who I am?'

'No!' snapped the girl.

'Good,' said the Irish girl and ran off.

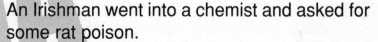

An Irishman went into a chemist and asked for some rat poison.

'I'm sorry, Sir,' said the chemist. 'We don't sell rat poison. Have you tried Boots?'

'I want to poison them, yer eejit,' replied the Irishman, 'not kick them to death!'

An Irishman was house-, pet- and granny-sitting for a family who had gone away on holiday. When the family returned the Dad asked how things were.

'Your cat is dead,' he said and the children started to cry.

'Nice one,' said the Dad to the Irishman. 'Couldn't you have been more tactful?'

'What do you mean?' asked the Irishman.

'Well you could have said something like, the cat was up on the roof when it slipped and fell to ground. You did all you could for it, but it died on the way to the vets.'

'Oh,' said the Irishman. 'I'll remember next time.'

'That's OK,' said the Dad. 'So how is granny?'

'Well,' started the Irishman, 'she was up on the roof and...'

The manager of the Dublin to Wicklow train was fed up with the last carriage always being vandalised. It was a porter at Dublin station that finally came up with the idea of leaving the last carriage off the train.

An Irishman had almost got the job as chief teaspoon stirrer on the building site, when the boss said he wanted to give him an intelligence test.

'What has one thumb, four fingers and is sometimes made of leather?' asked the boss. The Irishman thought long and hard before finally giving up.

'It's a glove,' said the boss. 'OK let's try another one. What has two thumbs, eight fingers and is made of leather?'
The Irishman thought even longer and harder and once again gave up.

'It's two gloves.' The boss nearly snapped. 'Look, I'll give you one more chance.'

'OK, I'll definitely get this one,' the Irishman said.

'This one is easy. Who is the Queen of England?'
The Irishman smiled. He knew this one all right.

'Now, that would be three gloves.'

Two Irishmen bought a tandem together, and they were out on their first ride. Everything was going well until they came to a very steep hill. The one on the back pedalled as hard as he could to reach top of the hill.

'That was a steep hill!' the Irishman said to his friend between gasping for breath.

'I know,' said the second Irishman. 'And it was lucky I kept the brakes on going up, otherwise we might have slid all the way back down it.'

Finnegan Beginnegan got a job painting the white lines in the middle of the road. At the end of his third day he was called into the manager's office.

'Now tell me Finnegan,' said the manager. 'How is it you painted three miles of lines on your first day, one mile on your second day, and less than 100 yards today?'

'It's not an easy job you know, boss,' said Finnegan, 'because each day it takes longer to walk back to the paint pot.'

An Irishman went to catch a bus and before he got on he asked the conductor how much it was to the High Street.

'£1.50,' the conductor said.

The Irishman thought that was far too expensive, so he ran behind the bus to save the pennies. After a couple of stops, he called to the conductor again and asked how much it was to the High Street.

'£3,' said the conductor.

'£3?' said the Irishman. 'But it was only £1.50 when I last asked.'

'This bus is going the other way.'

The Doctor was amazed after he had examined an Irishman, who had come in complaining of stomach pains.

'You're not going to believe this,' said the doctor, 'but you're pregnant.'

'You're joking!' replied the Irishman, a man in his forties. 'What will the neighbours say? I'm not even married!'

An Irishman had never played golf before, but he was invited by a business colleague to play at an exclusive club. On the first tee, he took a couple of practice swings then hit the ball. The ball sailed through the air and went straight in the hole. On the second tee, he belted the ball and got a hole in one again. He did it yet again on the third and fourth hole. On the fifth he hit the ball and sliced it widely. The ball hit some trees, bounced back out and hit a passing golf buggy, fell on to the green, rolled past the hole and up the green, then trickled back and plopped into the hole.

'Oh bejabers,' said the Irishman to his stunned partner. 'I thought I'd missed it that time.'

An Irishman was on holiday in Devon when he saw farmer loading up a truck with manure.

'What are you going to do with that?' the Irishman asked.

'I's gonna spread it on me strawberries,' said the farmer.

'Cor, you English are strange,' laughed the Irishman. 'We like cream on ours.'

An Irish priest walked into his church and saw a little girl sitting in one of the pews crying.

'What's the matter sweetheart?' asked the priest.

The little girl pointed up to the sky and sobbed.

'My Mammy and Da are up there and they've left me all alone!'

'Oh don't worry, child,' said the priest in reassuring tones. 'They are with the angels.'

'No they're not!' said the little girl. 'They're stripping the lead off the roof.'

There was a knock on an Irishman's front door and he opened it to see a man with some leaflets and a Bible.

'Excuse me, Sir,' the man said, 'but would you like to become a Jehovah's Witness?'

'Oh I don't think so,' said the Irishman. 'I didn't even see the accident.'

Two old Irishmen were sitting on a park bench having a chat about their hearing aids.

'The one I'm wearing is a state of the art digital sound enhancement system, with a range of half a mile, it doesn't hiss and can receive signals in 5.1 surround sound and Dolby logic. If you flick a switch you can even pick up the radio,' one of them said.

'That's amazing,' said the other Irishman.

'How much did it cost?'

'Half past three,' replied the old man.

The doctor rang an Irishwoman to see how she was doing with the pills he had prescribed for her bad back.

'Oh not too bad, doctor,' she said, 'but I do have a bit of a problem.'

'What's that?' asked the doctor.

'On the label it says take once after a bath.'

'That's right,' said the doctor. 'What's the problem?'

'Well,' said the Irishwoman. 'It's very tough going drinking all that bath water.'

'That's a strange looking dog,' Shamus said to the Stranger who came into the bar. 'What is it?'

'It's a long-nosed, long-tailed, short-legged terrier,' said the Stranger.

'I bet you £50 that my dog here could beat yours in a fight,' said Shamus, indicating the large Wolfhound that sat at his feet.

The Stranger took up the offer and the fight began. Within seconds Shamus's Wolfhound was dead.

'Wow, that dog can fight!' said Shamus, handing over the money. 'What did you say it was called?'

'A long-nosed, long-tailed, short-legged terrier.' replied the Stranger. 'But some people call it a crocodile.'

An Irishman was trying to make his own cider.

'How's it going?' asked his mate.

'Not too bad,' replied the Irishman, 'but it's a heck of a job squeezing the juice out of the woodpeckers.'

An Irishman had joined the army and was in the queue to get his kit.

'I don't know any of my sizes. I'm going to look a right eejit.'

'Don't worry,' said the guy in front. 'You're a little bit bigger than me, so when I say a measurement, you just say the next number.' The Quartermaster snapped at the guy and the Irishman in turn.

'Boots?'

'Seven,' said the guy.

'Eight,' said the Irishman.

'Trousers?'

'Thirty-four,' said the guy.

'Thirty-five,' said the Irishman.

'Shirt collar?'

'Fourteen,' said the guy.

'Fifteen,' said the Irishman.

'And finally hat size!' the Quartermaster bellowed.

'Six and seven eighths,' said the guy.

'Nine, ten, eleven,' said the Irishman.

An Irishman was queuing up at a ticket office in a train station.

'I'd like a return ticket please.'

'Where to?' asked the ticket sales woman.

'Back here, you stupid woman!' replied the Irishman.

'My granddad was burnt in a fire yesterday,' an upset Irishman told his friend.

'Was it bad?' he asked.

The Irishman wiped a tear from his eye. 'They don't mess about at that crematorium.'

'My husband never takes me out,' the Irishwoman moaned to her friend.

'Why ever not?' asked her friend.

'He says that it would be wrong of him to be seen out with a married woman.'

Mary opens her newspaper one morning and is surprised to see that according to the obituary column, she had died a few days ago. Dumbfounded, she phones up Colleen.

'Have you read the paper today?' Mary asks.

'No.'

'Well it says in there that I've died!' Mary shrieks.

'Are you sure?' questions Colleen.

'Of course I'm sure!'

There's a short silence on the phone and then...

'So Mary, where *are* you calling from?'

After months of planning and scheming, an Irishman had to give up his idea of robbing the local bank.

No matter how hard he tried, the tights only came up to his neck.

An English kid, a Scottish laddie and an Irish scallywag came across an enchanted playground. They knew it was enchanted because there was a leprechaun looking after it.

'The slide is a magical slide,' the leprechaun declared. 'Whatever you shout out as you slide down, will be at the bottom when you arrive.

The English kid went first and shouted out 'Playstations.' And sure enough he landed in amongst a gigantic pile of Playstations and games.

The Scottish laddie went next and he shouted out 'DVDs' and he landed in a big pile of DVDs.

Finally it was the turn of the Irish scallywag. He climbed to the top of the ladder, full of ideas. As he slid down, he screamed at the top of his voice.

'Weeeeeeee!'

An Irishwoman was nearing the end of her life. As her husband comforted her on her deathbed she had some wise words for him.

'You've been a wonderful husband to me. When I'm gone I want you to find another woman, get married and enjoy yourself. In fact I'd like you to give your new wife all my old clothes, especially my expensive dresses.'

'Darling, that's a wonderful gesture,' whispered the husband. 'But I can't do that!'

'I understand,' said the Irishwoman.

'No you don't,' said the husband. 'She's two sizes smaller than you.'

Kitty was angry when Joe opened the front door one night, staggered over the step, tripped on the hall mat and fell on the floor at her feet in a drunken mess.

'I've had enough of this!' she screamed. 'Why do you have to keep on coming home from that pub half drunk?'

'I always run out of money,' mumbled Joe.

McGinty used to go everywhere on his donkey. One day he went to his local pub for a shandy. When he came out, his donkey had been covered in green paint. McGinty stormed back into the pub.

'Which one of you eejits has painted my donkey green?'
Big Mick stood up. Now Mick was big and tough, the sort of guy who made King Kong look skinny.

'I did!' bellowed Big Mick. 'What about it?'
McGinty was petrified and looked up at Big Mick.

'Well I thought you'd like to know that the first coat is dry.'

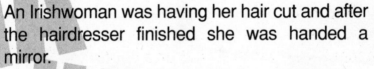

An Irishwoman was having her hair cut and after the hairdresser finished she was handed a mirror.

'Have a look and let me know what you think?' said the hairdresser.
The Irishwoman looked.

'It's very nice, but do you think I could have it a bit longer at the back?'

Paddy wanted to prove that not all Irishmen were thick. He went up to a shepherd in a field full of sheep and put on an English accent.

'Ere mate, if I can guess the exact number of sheep what you have in this field, can I take one home?'

The shepherd agreed.

'OK,' said Paddy, 'let's have a look. Right! There's 347 sheep in this field.'

'That's right,' said the shepherd.

'And now if you don't mind, mate, I'll have one of your sheep.'

'You're Irish aren't you?'

'How can you tell?' asked Paddy surprised.

'Could I have my dog back?'

'Did you hear about the Irishman who bought a house boat?'

'Really?'

'He drowned last week.'

'What happened?'

'He tried to add a basement.'

A scientist had made a lie detector chair. He designed it so that whoever sat it in would receive an electric shock if they told a lie. He took it to a little village to show it off.

'Who would like to try it?' he asked the assembled crowd.

'I will!' said an Irishman.
The scientist helped the Irishman to try the chair out for size. 'What do you think?'

The Irishman said, 'Well, I think...' And the chair gave him an electric shock.

Dr Mick E. Taker wasn't Ireland's greatest surgeon.

'Mr Devine, I've got some good news and some bad news for you.'

'What's the bad news, Doc?' asked Mr Devine.

'As you know, you were to have a leg amputated. Well, I'm afraid I cut off the wrong leg.'

'Oh dear,' said Mr Devine.

'So what's the good news?' Dr Taker smiled.

'Your bad leg is getting better.'

A fancy dress party was in full swing when there was a knock at the door. The host opened it and there was an Irishman with a girl on his back.

'What have you come as?' asked the host.

'A tortoise,' replied the Irishman.

'But why have you got that girl on your back?'

'That's Michelle,' smiled the Irishman.

Now I'm not saying that he was the laziest Irishman in the Ireland, but he was the only person I knew who would flush bread down the toilet to feed the seagulls at the seaside.

'So what was the result of the big match you went to see?' Dawn asked Shaun.

'It was nil–nil,' Shaun told her.

'Oh?' said Dawn. 'What was the score at half time?'

'I don't know,' replied Shaun. 'The bus was late, so I missed the first half.'

An Irishman went into his local DIY shop to return a chainsaw he had recently bought.

'What's the matter with it?' asked the assistant.

'It's not very good,' said the Irishman. 'I had a job clearing some trees and this thing was useless. I only chopped two trees down all day.'

'Let's have a look at it then,' said the assistant taking the chainsaw and pulling the cord so it screamed into life.

The Irishman jumped out of his skin. 'What's that noise?'

An Irishman stood up in the bar and started to sing:

'I'm proud to be an Irishman,
I'm proud to be an Irishman,
I'm proud to be an Irishman,
I'm proud to be an I.. .R...
I... .er... S ...erm..?
Oh I'm proud to be an
Irishman!'

An Irish girl goes to the doctor and tells him that her body hurts wherever she touches it. The doctor is puzzled and asks her to show him. The Irish girl touches her knee and screams in pain. She touches her head and screams in pain. In fact whatever part of her body she touches, she screams.

'I can see the problem,' said the doctor.

'What is it?' the Irish girl asks nervously. 'Have I got a terminal illness?'

'Oh no,' reassures the doctor, 'but you have broken your finger.'

An Irish wolf was prowling through the forest looking for food. Suddenly there was a loud snap! followed by a yelp, as the wolf got caught in a bear trap.

In desperation to escape, the wolf chewed off three of its legs, but was still stuck.

An Irishman was on the Antiques Roadshow and one of the experts was looking at what he had brought in.

'And you say you found this in your loft?' said the expert.

'That's right Sir,' the Irishman replied. 'It's been up there for years.'

The expert shook his head. 'Well I'm afraid that it isn't worth a penny.'

'Why's that?' asked the Irishman.

'It's your water tank.'

'Hey Boylan,' called Moylan over the garden fence one summer's afternoon. 'Are you using your lawn mower today?'

'Yeah,' replied Boylan.

'Great!' said Moylan. 'Then can I borrow your golf clubs? You won't need them as you're going to be busy.'

At a school assembly, a doctor was giving a lecture on the evils of drink.

He put two glasses on the table in front of him and a big fat worm in each. He poured water into one glass and Irish whiskey into the other. The worm in the glass of water bobbed about happily, but the worm in the whiskey died immediately.

'So what does this little demonstration prove to you all?' asked the doctor.
O'Malley called from the back of the room:

'If you suffer from worms, drink a lot of whiskey.'

Two Irishmen had spent a successful day fishing from a boat. Just before they set off for shore, one of them painted a cross on the side of the boat.

'What you doing?' asked the second Irisman.

'By doing this, next time we can come back to the same spot to fish.'

'Oh you are an eejit,' said the second Irishman. 'We might not get the same boat again.'

A little Irish girl was talking to her little sister.

'You know Father Christmas?' said the litte Irish girl.

'Yes,' answered her little sister.

'Well, I think it's Daddy.'

'Why?'

'Because he never shaves and only works one day a year.'

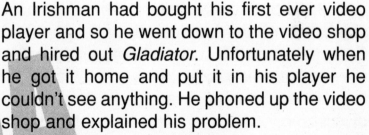

An Irishman had bought his first ever video player and so he went down to the video shop and hired out *Gladiator*. Unfortunately when he got it home and put it in his player he couldn't see anything. He phoned up the video shop and explained his problem.

The clerk was very helpful.

'Is your television tuned into the right channel?' he asked.

'What television?'

It was lunchtime and an Irishman was sitting high up in the scaffolding with his lunchbox.

'Oh not cheese sandwiches again. I hate them,' he said to his mate. The next day the same thing. This went on all through the week, and on Thursday the Irishman said to his mate, 'If I get cheese sandwiches tomorrow, I'm going to throw myself off this scaffolding.'

Come Friday, the Irishman opens his lunchbox, sees the cheese sandwiches and promptly throws himself off the scaffolding.

The Foreman and the Irishman's mate stand round the splattered body and the Foreman says, 'It's such a shame, all this over cheese sandwiches.'

'I know, and he always used to make his own.'

Two Irish pilots had just landed their plane for the first time at Shannon Airport.

'That was a good landing,' said the first pilot, 'considering how short this runway is.'

'I know, and would you look how wide it is?' said the co-pilot.

An Irishman was working so hard on the building site, carrying a massive hod load of bricks up and down a ladder that it was beginning to worry his friend.

'Hey,' said the friend, 'don't work too hard! It doesn't look good for the rest of us if the Site Foreman sees.'

'Oh don't panic about that,' said the Irishman. 'I've got him fooled. It's the same load of bricks each time.'

An Irishman was in a restaurant and had called the waiter over.

'Excuse me,' he said. 'The peas with this meal are disgusting. They're hard as rocks.'

The waiter picked up a spare fork and scooped up some peas from the Irishman's plate, put them in his mouth and ate them.

'They seem perfectly soft to me,' said the waiter snootily.

'Well they would be,' replied the Irishman. 'I've been chewing them for the last half hour.'

A little Irish boy came home from school early one day because the boy next to him in class had been smoking. His mum was livid and rang up the school to complain.

'Why is it,' she raged down the phone, 'that my son gets sent home because the boy next to him is smoking? It's disgraceful.'

'But Mrs O'Donnell,' said the head teacher. 'It was your son who set him on fire!'

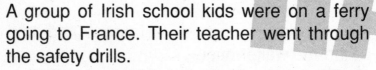

A group of Irish school kids were on a ferry going to France. Their teacher went through the safety drills.

'OK class, let's just check what we do in emergency. If one of you falls overboard, what do the others shout?'

'Child overboard!' they all shouted in unison.

'That's right,' smiled the teacher. 'And what would you shout if a teacher fell overboard?'

Little Kenny put up his hand. 'Excuse Miss, which one?'

A pilot was flying in a hot air balloon and was lost somewhere over Limerick. He looked down and saw a farmer out in a field and shouted down.

'Hello there, where am I?'
The Irish farmer looked up.

'Oh you can't fool me, you're in that little basket.'

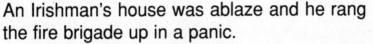

An Irishman's house was ablaze and he rang the fire brigade up in a panic.

'Me house is on fire, me house is on fire. Help me!' he screamed down the phone.

'Don't panic, Sir,' said the operator. 'We will be on our way. We just need to know how we can get to your house?'

'Well I suggest that big red truck with the flashing blue light,' replied the Irishman.

An American tourist arrived in Wicklow and asked a local to show him the biggest building in the town.

'There you are,' said the local pointing to a large house. 'The biggest house in Wicklow.'

The American looked at the house and laughed. 'You call that a building, Buddy? Back home we have buildings ten times the size of that.'

'That I don't doubt!' The local smiled. 'That's the local lunatic asylum.'

An Irishman went to see his doctor.

'What is it?'

'It's me right arm, Doc,' said the Irishman. 'It aches so much.'

The doctor took a look at the Irishman's arm.

'It's old age I'm afraid.'

'Old age?' replied the Irishman. 'My left arm is the same age. How come that one doesn't ache as well?'

Paddy had nasty accident at work and got his ear cut off and he couldn't find it. Finally Thaddy picked up the ear from behind a machine.

'Here it is, Paddy!'
Paddy looked at the severed ear. 'That's not my ear, Thaddy! Mine had a pencil behind it.'

Did you hear the one about the Irish girl who went to the Doctor's?

'Doctor, I don't know what's the matter with me recently,' she said. 'Some days I just don't know where I am, at all, at all?'
'Fares please!' shouted the bus conductor.

An Irish mugger stopped a man in a street and said.

'Give me all your money or else.'

'Or else, what?' asked the man.

'Look, don't confuse me,' said the mugger. 'This is the first time I've done this.'

'Doc, I feel really strange,' an Irishman told his doctor. 'I keep feeling that I can see into the future.'

'That's very interesting,' said the doctor. 'When did these strange feelings start?'

'Next Thursday.'

Did you hear the one about the Irish farmer who stood out in a paddock for three days?

Apparently he wanted to win the Nobel Peace Prize and to do that he was told he had to be outstanding in his field!

An Irishman went for a job as a miner and at the interview was asked what he knew about gas regulations. The Irishman thought long and hard and then answered, 'Well I know its mark 7 for Toad in the Hole.'

'I just had a loft extension,' boasted an Irishman.

'I bet that was expensive,' said his friend.

'It was,' answered the Irishman, 'and it really upset the man in the flat above.'

Now we're not saying that he was the smelliest man in Ireland, but one day he decided to put some 'odour-eaters' in his shoes. Five minutes later he had disappeared.

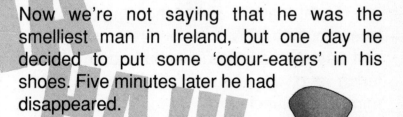

Did you hear the one about the two Irish boys who got a sledge for Christmas?

One of them used it for going down the hill and the other used it for going up!

Did you hear the one about the Irishman who fell into the grave he had just dug?

He wasn't actually a gravedigger. He was just filling in for a friend.

'Right lads,' said the building site foreman, 'one more thing before you start your first day. All you lads can have one hour for lunch and all you Irish lads have fifteen minutes for lunch.'

'Ach, that's not fair!' said one of the Irish lads. 'How comes they get an hour for lunch and we only get fifteen minutes?'

'So we don't have to keep retraining you.'

Did you hear the one about the Irishman who was sacked from the banana packing factory?

The boss said to only pack the perfect bananas so he threw away all the bent ones!

A young Irishman runs into a bar and shouts, 'Call me a doctor! Will someone please call me a doctor?'

'What's wrong?' asks the barman. 'Are you ill?'

'No,' replies the Irishman. 'I've just graduated from medical school!'

Mary was staring at Colleen as she put lipstick on her forehead.

'Colleen, what are you doing?' asked a confused Mary.

'My boyfriend is taking me out tonight and he said that I need to make my mind up.'

An Irishman was complaining to his friend about his constipation.

'It's awful,' the Irishman said. 'I can be on the loo for hours and hours.'

'Do you take anything?' asked his friend.

'Oh yeah, I always take me newspaper and maybe a book.'

Cath O'Keely went into her local James Bond themed hairdressers called 'Dye Another Day' and talked to Maurice, the head hair-dresser.

'Maurice, I want you to make me look ten years younger.'

'I'm sorry Mrs O'Keely,' said Maurice, 'this is a hairdresser's, not a time machine.'

Two Irish boys were boasting in class.

'I ran the hundred metres in five seconds,' claimed one.

'No way!' scoffed his friend. 'That's less than the world record.'

'Well,' said the first Irish boy, 'I know a short cut.'

'Of course you all know why God invented whiskey?' the Irish professor asked his class. Dillon, a bright student put up his hand and said, 'Sir, was it to prevent us Irish from ruling the world?

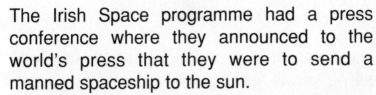

The Irish Space programme had a press conference where they announced to the world's press that they were to send a manned spaceship to the sun.

'But you can't do that!' said one reporter. 'The sun is so hot that anyone who went anywhere near it would be burned alive.'

'Ah, but our scientists have thought of that,' said the leader of the programme smugly. 'That's why we are going at night.'

Did you hear the one about the Irishman who bought a piece of wrapping paper that was 1 inch by 30 metres so that he could send his Mammy a new washing line?

Unfortunately she sent it back because her garden wasn't long enough!

Mary was on the phone to her friend, Betty telling her all about her new digital television.

'Oh I can't get digital television where I am,' said Betty.

'Where's that?' asked Mary.

'In the garden,' replied Betty.

An Irishman was walking in a park and he saw another man throw a stick into a lake. The man's dog walked on the water, picked up the stick and brought it back. The man did this a couple of times while the Irishman watched in amazement. Finally he went up to the man.

'So, when are you going to teach your dog to swim?'

A television reporter was interviewing a man for making a brave citizen's arrest.

'Well, the police couldn't do it, the Paramedics couldn't do it, and the fire brigade couldn't do it. How did you get the one-armed Irish cat burglar out of that tree?'

'Oh it was easy,' said the man. 'I just waved to him.'

An Irishman was driving down a road, swerving all over the place. Finally the police stopped him.

'Oh thank goodness you're here,' he said to the policeman. 'I was driving down this road when all of a sudden this tree appeared in front of me. I swerved to avoid it, then another one appeared. I missed that one. Then another one appeared and another one and...'

'Sir,' said the policeman. 'May I suggest you take that pine scented air freshener down from your mirror?'

An Irishman walks into a pub and is surprised to see another Irishman up at the bar who he recognises.

'Terence O'Milligan,' says the Irishman. 'I haven't seen you in years. Haven't you changed? You used to be thin, but now you're fat. You used to be ginger, but now you're bald. You used to be clean-shaven, but now you've got a beard. I wouldn't have known you!'

The other Irishman looks at him in a somewhat confused state. 'My name's Michael O'Rourke.'

'Would you look at that,' exclaims the Irishman. 'You've even changed your name!'